DEER *on the* PARKWAY

JAMES FRAZIER

Library of Congress Control Number: 2021901394

HARDBACK: 978-1-954673-63-2
PAPERBACK: 978-1-954673-62-5
EBOOK: 978-1-954673-64-9

Ordering Information:

For orders and inquiries, please contact:
1-888-404-1388
www.goldtouchpress.com
book.orders@goldtouchpress.com

Printed in the United States of America

INTRODUCTION

At the beginning of human activity people lived their lives on earth in accordance with natural rules; half in light and half in darkness. For most of our kind there has been an umbra over hitherto unheard of adventures. A universal shadow has lingered over the deeds of mankind.

Today leads a new era in what can be said about our exploits. With revelations coming to light on these pages will come a transparent bowl of explication. Our source of wisdom will be the history and lore of all things retold.

As these stories have come to me in parts over the course of my life, they may at times seem disjointed or non-equidistant to some readers. Be assured nonetheless that by their revelation enlightenment can be attained.

In modest resignation to that which created me, I pay homage to the emergence of Aries; sign of the Ram. When he sets out across melting skies and breathes new life into the season of spring, I too am given breadth to renew my course. As certain as Leap Year has an extra day, I promise that all events occurred in place and time as I will devise to you.

I

All through the ages we have been told by wise men of why and how all things came about. We have chosen mostly to accept those interpretations as true; sometimes without factual evidence to support them. Ironically, we tend to look for affirmation of what has been passed down to us in order to maintain our ways.

Some translations of our own history and lore have left us enriched and forever blessed. Others have divested us of the strength and spiritual significance that feed our cultures. Over the ages we have filtered our ideals to suit that which needs to be achieved. Our wants and needs, our goals, our ambitions are all part of a greater drive.

We believe that events of the past can be individualized to the point of being separate from nearby or related occurrences. Yet, we as members of a global society have to make all things fit one divine scheme. Only then will we move on to the next great era in the evolution of mankind.

However we dissect past events there is always the matter of whether or not we are better for it. Would a different outcome have benefitted us more?

Certainly in many ways society could be better with different views of some historic occurrences. Perhaps men have been overzealous in relating what has happened in their own aspects of the world. Yet most people in our times are comfortable that what we know as the truth; is true.

We can conclude that significant events happen the way that witnesses say they do. We can also summarize that a fair degree of isolation takes place in their unraveling. That is to say that, much speculation is involved. Are we therefore to conclude that significant events are isolated in meaning? Based on our human abilities and digressions the answer has to be; no!

We know that events in our cultures require not only reason, but motivation as well. Without motivation, why even take the first step? Without it there is no reason to summon up the energy. We can say with certainty that whatever happens in our existence, mankind is motivated by events that are more broad in scope than what he has experienced in his individual life. Let us also say that it is unwise to draw philosophical conclusions from things that are happening around us.

The world of man is complicated by language. The use of which is made problematic by our unique ability to remember and to forget. If we can draw any proven conclusion, it is that what man has done and what we have heard is by divine design.

II

It is in light of these reconciliations that I pay homage to the concert of events which found me in the situation of having to live in a Day Rate Shelter. I am not embarrassed or angry. Nor do I bear any ill-will from this matter; I am simply, at this place. I make no excuses, nor infer any flaws. Here at this place for the homeless; at this time: the end of the old and the beginning of the new millennium, I have found my otherwise home. The residents here are my new temporary family.

Having recently lost my parents and having been displaced from my childhood friends, I was careless with my planning and somewhat fell into economic stress. There is a higher calling for me, but that must come in my next chosen steps. I intend to take things one step at a time. I am confined by these elements and I must accept my station. From here I am content to work on improving my world.

This new family, for want of a better description, carries the trait of being unpretentious. It is a tragic quality in all human beings, but seems to be compounded in this lot. All of our great societies have cloaked themselves in some sort of pretext. The same can be said about the values and mores of my upbringing. That is not to say that I am pretentious. It is to say that the qualities of my new family are some, which have been missing from my experiences.

III

To the extent that I have experienced many and various situations, there is no cause for alarm nor reason to defer any previous goals. My ambitions are unchanged, albeit on a different course. Here, I may find out new things about he human animal, and yet not be impacted to distraction. For example, it will do no harm to learn vicariously, what equipment is best suited for camping in this or that part of the country. Information of this ilk may never prove of any value to me. Nevertheless, it does me no harm to retain it.

I am privy to a brand new set of rules of survival in this southern Georgia city where I was born. It allows my imagination to run freely, pealing away the ideals that my parents, teachers, peers and other authorities have so covetously vested in me.

At the same time, I know that I could never survive by any other lifestyle but hard work. I thought that I was well-educated enough to know about every condition of life. Being here though, teaches me that the less I know, the better I can function.

By this I man that, a good education is rooted in the interpretations of well- educated persons. Schools pass along a body of information which those of us who are lucky enough to receive it, voluntarily pass along to other lucky recipients. Not many scholars are motivated to change the system. We study long and hard, and we deduce ways to enforce what we know by adhering to our scholarship precisely.

Given a quick decision or hasty choice, the first reaction may not be one's own. Reaction based on scholarship may be totally different from reaction based on living near society's fringe. While educated persons find comfort in other educated persons, everyone at some point gets thrown a strange ball. If an individual has learned well enough, making the right call will come naturally.

I am confident enough to know that this situation will pass and fade into distant memory. I am also wise enough to know that what I take from these times must never be viewed lightly.

IV

My intent here is to abide by the rules of the building and to assimilate myself as much as possible; and in so doing, to access the quality of being liked. And, conversely, to avoid being labeled as one of the lot. I can show the façade of listening, yet not hear a word they are saying.

Within a few days I learned that my capacity to endure hard work is greater than that of my two hundred or so brethren. I was soon getting calls from contractors to work on a daily basis.

I came to embrace the physical realm as a way of escaping emotional and mental stress. I have always played hard and studied hard. But up to now, I have never worked hard. I felt pleased with myself and with the way I was connected to all the implications of 'working with one's hands'. What I was not sure about though was where this road would lead.

Roads exist as surely as the world turns. A road is a road because it leads you to somewhere. I am hesitant as to where this road will lead essentially because I have given up some of my cares.

If I hold to these ways and not apply any thought to their significance I will see only the facades. See only what a tourist sees before hitting the road again.

V

Will the path that I am on open up new doors? And what will those doors pertain to: learning, social opportunities, openness? I believe that ultimately a road leads home.

Along the way there have to be distractions. It is what men have always had to contend with. That is why roads inspire streets, which inspire lanes, which lead to pathways, and so many other ways to leave the beaten path.

Being uncertain about your direction is not a safe status. A path can take you anywhere imaginable. It can even lead to another path. One must avoid if possible, ending up in an unplanned, unknown location. Additionally, the longer that a road extends, the more varied its significance.

This world of ours is very wide. Quite possibly I have seen the road I'm on before; only under different conditions.

In other words; roads that go north also go south. No matter the circumstances we must be able to face ourselves in the mirror and to reflect on what we are doing. We have to be familiar with ourselves and how we react under various conditions. If I hold to these streets, seeing only the facades there is the chance of being distracted beyond recovery. If I keep what I am doing in perspective, I can do the things that I know will help me stay on the right road. Then and only then; with graces from the divine, will my road as well hold the promise of a destination.

"Welcome to your new temporary home. We will be your new temporary family."

The weight of destiny for most people lies heavily upon their shoulders. We may achieve our goals, but have to be certain of how to go about it. Our moves are simple notions that have to be accepted by others. The destiny of one person has to be to the affectation of most people whose lives he will touch.

One cannot dissolve the etchings of ones past without affecting the lives of others. We owe an allegiance to our peers, even though our destinations may seem singular of purpose. Let us fill in the blanks of our hearts for personal reasons. But let us also navigate the maze of people who touch us along the way.

Where can we fix this line of reasoning? Is that other person on the same path as I? Or is that other person standing in my path? In order to realize our hopes we must be constantly aware of minute distinctions. The passing of time has shown us that difficult decisions have to be made. This world of ours is what shapes our destinies. It brings us night and day. It changes for new seasons. And it provides us with food and shelter. This earth is our natural home.

One's first act of responsibility is to define his own destiny. The next is to make a step along the way. Be it intellectual, as man is obligated to do, or instinctively, which can be equally forceful, we all view life in terms of what lies ahead.

To set one's dreams into motion is to set out into society. Thereupon, we might be assisted by traditional values. We can be guided by cultural morals, have family values, and be possessed of many skills learned from ceremonies, rituals, and lore. As we move forward and our responsibilities grow, all these ways take on diverse uses. The need for socialization becomes greater, placing more importance upon individual influence and success. In comparison to where we have come from, where we are going is getting a lot more complicated.

Let us not forget that we are also guided by human spirit. We follow those instinctive rules which apply to all of mankind. They tell us to be kind to our peers. And they imply other simple commandments which help our understanding. A reasonably intelligent person knows that he must reap what he sows; that he must honor his mother and father; and that only the strong survive.

II

I placed great importance upon my own upbringing as a way of dealing with the unforeseen situation that life had brought. If living in a day shelter is part of my divine destiny, then let it be. I know that I am fully prepared for whatever must befall. These conditions need not be an obstacle to my view of the world. Perhaps a detour; an opportunity perchance, to unearth some element in me that would elewise be unreachable.

And so it went on. Day after day for some time, until I realized that at least one elderly gentleman had some intelligent experiences to relate. His bed was under the one which I was assigned. He was given a lower bunk, as was every senior so they did not have to climb. Jean would speak every night in very worldly educated ways about his accomplishments. The men in neighboring beds usually found him boring with the non-stop palaver. But I always listened. At times I had to challenge the truthfulness of what he was saying. One night for example, he was talking about his skills as a member of the Canadian Olympic Team. It was all good until he divulged that he participated in the Games of 1942. That was the point at which I had to interrupt and remind him that there were no Games in that year because of the Great War. Jean then was more than glad to point out that he took part in the Winter Olympics, not the Summer Olympics. Those games according to Jean, indeed took place in that year.

Sometimes I found myself not well informed enough to dispute what he told us. I was not a participant in the Winter Games of '42, therefore, I could not address the issue of whether or not he was. As well, I was not inclined to go to a library and research his claim. I was at best, interested to listen to those stories as he said they took place.

Where do unproven stories end up? I wondered for a while if I was being guided by fantasies that someone else had forged. I rationalized that if the old man was fantasizing, then it was just as well to believe him as it were to not believe. Everything that he said was irrelevant, other than as being an interesting story. I could listen intently to every word being said, and yet not fall prey to a pack of lies. The events that he served up never required any proof. His versions of what happened were all that was needed. We would listen until no one was awake. If Jean sensed skepticism among any of the listening audience, he would adjust his story to suit what it was that we needed to hear. Before I could question him for example, about where his Quebec accent had gone, he was already telling us about the time his family moved across the border into New York state.

That circumstance was fine with me. It satisfied my curiosity about his Americanization. At the same time, Jean already knew that my grandparents are New Yorkers. The result I thought was that I would have a more sympathetic ear. Consequently I was on guard against any personal associations he might use to draw me into his babble. More often than not, we believed him. After all, he had nothing to gain by filling the air with embellished lies. Also, a person as smart as himself would have to have prevailed in life somewhere close to the way he portrays. My only problem was with his tenure here.

When I was not on guard, I could realize a kinship with his days and times; though, my earliest recollections go back thirty seven years or so. I can remember being at sports arenas with my uncles and older brothers up north. It all begins when I was less than five years old.

I recall meeting the professional ballplayers who were friends with my brothers. Although Jean's path and mine had never crossed until now, his upbringing and early life were not very different from my own. When I reflect on those times, they bring me great ease and comfort.

III-1

I used to look forward to visiting my grandparents every summer as a child. Changing location became part of my learning process. I have a core family which is based in the south, and an extended family based in the north.

Being with family is a part of childhood. The fact that my family is eight hundred miles apart did not deter us at all. Georgia to New York for my family and me is a natural destination. Not a trek, nor a move, nor even a tedious drive, it is a part of the way we are.

One might say that changing locations and travelling such distances is a symptom of instability. "Just stay in one place!" you might say. But for me, it comes by rote.

There is an inner stability that comes from being with family. Even if it means being on the road for twenty hours.

Having a reunion, being together, makes everything all worthwhile. The family as a group is its own destiny. No one member is as great as the whole. Whether you like or dislike a particular member, that person's status and duty to family does not change. As a member of our family, stability is in kind.

Whatever it takes to reaffirm the bond is worth every step of the way.

II

To be sure, my extended family is a great destiny. Being with them is being in familiar territory, though I travel so very far. Once there, it was as though I had never been any place else. I know the houses, streets, names, and faces like home. There were some differences in dialect and abruptness of manner. I was not shy at being there. I fit right in. My new attitudes would begin as soon as I fell in with my cousins. Sometimes the words I used were different. But our play and game objectives were always the same; having lots of fun. The environments were slightly different from the ones down south, but we enjoyed ourselves without hesitation.

When old times are reawakened I would fall right into my extended family ways. It was not as if I were in a strange city with strange people. I was the product of a long history of family tradition.

With any number of aunts, uncles, nephews, or cousins I would go out to play. I cannot recall for certain the name of the pool we went to, but I remember swimming. As well, I remember skating, playing with milk crates, and going to stores.

The streets and buildings seemed all too familiar. Nothing seemed to be wrong. Even when I wondered to myself sometimes if we the children were doing the right things, we always had lots and lots of fun.

As if by some divine design I made my way from one corner of the globe to another. Looking back, I can say that I was blessed. I never had to make guesses about my development. The worldliness which

I inherited gave me a broad perspective. I could address the intricate points of my southern home, and distinguish them from up north. I was a well rounded young person.

I realize also that when I am in Georgia, I can do this. And when I am in New York, I could do that.

The values that I reveal here cannot be applied to every person, and every family across the board. Still I set them hurtling meticulously over these pages. I am of the belief that reason and wealth of culture have been already given to me. Much of it by my parents, and still more by the choices which I have made over the years.

My lifestyles and ways are specific to me. I am guided by facility. My personal history has an aura. It surrounds me with its own atmosphere. This atmosphere works most comfortably for me. Another person can behave like me, sound like me, and look like me. But only I can be me. Everything that I know about myself tells me that I am the right person to live this life which I was born to live.

I know as well, who I am by the ways in which others perceive me. I am judged by my height, weight, color, creed, and any number of attitudinal ways that I am capable of showing. It is my choice alone as to when I should act on one attitude or another.

I am always aware of my surroundings. I can sense when the environment is favorable for me. I have always been able to make the correct choices when it comes to exploiting what's in front of me. By the same token, that wariness of my surroundings has trained me to be alert for other options. In times when things are unfavorable for me, I can handle myself very well.

My decisions are genuine because so much is at stake. I make those instinctive choices, which are a component of my everyday life. The traditions which I value from the past as well as for the future, all have their cause and effect. If I believed that I were a negative, or brutal, accusative kind of person I would address many issues in that manner. But according to the standards of my family and myself I will always approach my issues in a relevant, studious, and thoughtful way.

All that considered, it is understandable how I can handle my current situation with an attitude of tolerance. Where I might find one resident interesting and bright, I may find another abrasive and dim witted. My ideas about making a comfortable way of living in this shelter seem very different from some others who reside here.

An example of what I am referring to would be the crude conversations of my neighbor, Big Bobby. He kept boasting loudly one night about the time when he had three orgasms in one hour with the same fat woman. The more descriptive he became, the more irritated I got. While most others roared with laughter, I could hear Jean snoring.

That seemed like a good idea! Taking my cue from him, I began to snore as well. I could still hear Big Bobby's gibberish but with deaf ears.

IV-I

As a matter of nature, each man has formed a persona: one that should be suited to his well being. There are set ways which are acted out no matter what the situation. Our behaviors are not a consequence of choice. Each person must fulfill the personal tasks which are bestowed upon him. Our souls are like fingerprints; everyone is different, yet each is a recognizable pattern. Whether we like that pattern or not, it gives us our traits, and they define each person for the duration of his existence.

The conditions for each man's life are made for him at the point of his conception. The choices made by him as a person are results of those genetic conditions. Inevitably he is challenged with issues of class, wealth, political allegiance and so on which help or hinder is choices. Nevertheless, a person will make those decisions that are most relevant to his own satisfactions.

Of course there are outside influences in our development. As we go on our private ways there are sanctions placed upon us by rule of law. The greater part of our behaviors must conform. In order to avoid being anti- establishment, we learn early in life how to streamline our choices. We are taught the consequences of misbehavior. As we strive toward our personal goals, each of us must consider his responsibilities to society, and its laws.

We cannot make random choices in life. Man is set apart from other creatures on this planet by his intellect and reason. We put all things into intellectual perspective. Part of that is to compromise our hopes and dreams as they pertain to the unknown.

A person will cradle himself over time in a sort of intellectual comfort zone. It is a zone which he becomes reluctant to leave without strong reasons. But because he is a human being, he must at least wonder what else is 'out there'.

It is not imperative that a person change his ways. Yet he can hope to achieve greater things. In other words, one might ask oneself "...am I the best that I can be?" If so, there is no need for panic. It is a valid question to wrestle with. We have the ability and tendency to look at things that are not directly in front of us. Change is sometimes good; and sometimes, if only for change's sake.

We must remain comfortable with a state of mind. Often times too much wonderment is not good. To follow a whim as an upstart, can be as harmful as to follow an instinct. A rational person is one who can see that hopes and dreams are more often than not, just that. A small step towards a goal can effect not only oneself, but many others in ones path. Thus, the wisest dream is not necessarily the wisest move.

We become set in our ways for various reasons. By definition we are small, but significant parts of a whole. We consider ourselves as being reasonable when we mitigate personal ways to meet the needs of society at-large. The greatest way we can serve is by staying within the nomenclature.

People always find comfort in sanctuary. Persons who for any reason, cannot avail themselves of the comforts of home, truly know what discomfort is.

A Day Shelter can be a home. For someone who is eligible to stay there year-round, there is actually no distinction. The shelter that I am calling home 'temporarily', caters to most basic needs. A long term resident can say that all of his basic needs are being met. There is no need to pursue other ends if in fact, one functions better in this type of sanctuary.

One conclusion which I have drawn is that happiness does not have to relate to luxury. The line I have drawn before me, which defines a happy home is a blurry one indeed.

II

I find myself now as actually counter productive to this situation. My hard working, well mannered, self-supporting behavior, is not the norm. Yet I have no other way of manifesting myself here except through hard work and positive thinking. To accuse other brethren of 'not' being productive is not my style. Suffice to say that I have exposed myself to a side of human nature that I have not personally been exposed to before.

With faith in ourselves we learn to address the world we see. We learn from others before us how to socialize. We embellish on what we learn to facilitate some characteristic traits. Each man is one of a kind. His personal development can only happen once: as in a vacuum. That which has shaped me is different from that which has shaped you.

Every man has to define his own space, and what can be done therein. His choices are his alone. Someone who appears to act weird, may have every reason to do so. Unless that person is a danger to himself, there is no reason to think any less of him as of any other person.

A clear thinking person is one who will thrive in his environment; an environment where day to day choices are easy to make. As always he is surrounded and comforted by others of a similar kind. One must take advantage of social ventures wherever they arise. And one must be confident in his own abilities to fit into the scheme of things.

A person becomes comfortable with himself when he is at ease in his environment. Socializing on familiar terms means that one is at home with his way of doing things. As such, his goals in life can be acted upon. One can think and move freely towards his aims with those tools which are available to him. Under conditions which one man perceives a stumbling block, another may see a stepping stone.

III

One evening I returned to the shelter from a hard day's work. I was met by a resident manager. He was requesting that I do another week on the chore list. I reminded him that I had just completed my week on the list and that it was someone else's turn. He said it was Ivory's turn, but that Ivory had been involved in an accident. Ivory had fallen down the East door steps and injured himself. He had been taken to the clinic for observation. He would remain there over the following three days.

I agreed to cover for him. Every evening upon my return, I mopped the showers, the West hallways, and the West dormitories. I didn't mind however, at all. I prefer a clean building. I did what I had to do to keep it that way.

A few days later I saw Ivory sitting on the patio with a group of friends. The guys, including Big Bobby were just being themselves. They were hanging out talking in gibberish, and just laughing themselves into hysteria. I asked Ivory if he was doing okay. He said yes so I simply went on my way.

This was typical, everyday activity. Looking back at it from a different perspective, I have the notion that they were laughing at me. It never dawned on me at the time, but I recognize now that Ivory had skillfully pressed his chore assignments onto me.

Up to that point I had no reason to perceive myself as being used. First of all I could not understand why anyone would need to bail out of a simple chore; especially when it meant that he was doing his fair share. Secondly; why would anyone perpetrate a ruse upon his brotherly neighbor? Predictably as a result, I was not immediately able to to recognize what the deal was. Moreover, I can say that I did not care about the small games people played.

IV

I have inherited one of my father's most enduring traits. It is that he and I are persons who are not easily forgotten. We linger in the psyche of those persons with whom we have any exchanges. I am not nearly as outgoing. But neither he nor I could ever be mistaken for someone else. I learned early in life that managing my own affairs would be a specific task. I don't blend in easily, and like my father, I will usually get the last word. Additionally, I never wanted for much as a child. My parents had the means to cater to my every need.

With long hours of work at his shop, his unwavering devotion to his church, and my siblings, I didn't get much individual attention. However, I never let that become an issue. There were always plenty of people around to keep me distracted. And whatever the crowd, the majority of circumstances always come back to me. One summer as a small child, for example, my family was bringing me back to Georgia after spending a few weeks in New York. We stopped at the Maryland House outside Baltimore for lunch. A female employee greeted my father. She looked at me and said "Hey! This little guy passed through here last month!"

I do not recall nowadays what specifically went through my mind. What I do recall is that I was astonished. Up to that point I viewed myself as insignificant. I was a little boy who was considered as good, smart, handsome, and obedient. For a total stranger living in a faraway place to have remembered me was something very special. Not to be mistaken for politeness, she actually knew me.

Meanwhile, my mother was giving me a look that said, "There now, you see? That's what I was trying to tell you!" The waitress was referring to the time a few weeks earlier when my older brother had brought me to New York. It meant that I, and I alone was the focus of her attention.

That particular truck stop was already one of my favorites. Being recognized there by the pretty lady, only added to its allure. You might say also that it added to my own!

For the rest of the summer, our telephone was abuzz with how popular I was becoming. For some reason, whenever my father spoke on long distance calls, he could be heard throughout our house.

Those were the days in my life when horizons began to expand. I was realizing that being prepared to have friends both in Georgia and in New York, was not enough. I knew that I needed to be sharp enough to meet people in those places and everywhere else in between.

I could no longer do what I overheard my mother say I was doing.

According to her, I stared at the waitress with my mouth wide open.

VI

The Maryland House episode is one of many moments branded into my psyche. I also have vivid fixations with an Olympic Marathon runner. It has to do with my youthful interests in sports. My brothers and I never missed watching the Olympic Games. That summer we became transfixed by the Ethiopian distance runner Abebe Bekele. We looked on in silence as he ran through the streets in his bare feet.

There is also a vivid recollection that I have of being transfixed by the actor Marlon Brando in his portrayal of Don Corleone. We were watching the movie 'The Godfather'. I can still feel the anguish he felt as he tried and failed to steer his son away from his own violent path.

Those episodes however, are impersonal. They arise from media events set up for my entertainment. They do not apply to my development. The Maryland House event, with all its innocence guided me to a higher plane. It represents an age when I decided that socializing goes beyond my immediate family. It spurred images in my mind of a larger world: a world where outsiders also play a role. I have to be responsive to persons even though I might not know their names.

There had to be some sort of dialogue, I thought, that is acceptable across the board. Surely there is some way of speaking, or behaving that gets you out of embarrassing situations.

I remember thinking, "How would my father have dealt with things?" And "What was it actually that my mother was trying to tell me?" But alas, I did not know! I had gone as far as I could with the notion of being the invisible child. I was becoming familiar to other people at other stops along the way. I could not allow myself to dwell however, on personalities. I had a destination, and the most important thing was getting there safely.

I identified the bond between myself and those other persons. They were faces along the way! They had no say in where I was going, nor when I got there, or who else I met. Their lives were not tied to mine in any complicated way. The one and only thing that tied them to me was 'reception'. To them, I was a traveler! Their contacts with me would never go beyond the functions of saying hello and goodbye. They would sell to us whatever we needed, then wish us a safe voyage.

Yet their roles cannot be overlooked. They offered us kindness and accommodations. Traveling along the highways can be an empty, feral pursuit. Those friendly hosts are valuable cultural intermediaries. People in Virginia are different from people we meet in South Carolina. But they are not so different that we cannot understand each other. We seemed to always have an easy transition with our hosts; those persons we meet along the way.

It was a difficult period for me. Transitions never come easily. I somehow overcame the inwardness which had carried me so far in my young life. My outgoing personality was a well considered choice for me. I was obliged to greet those persons whom I met on the road. I let them know that I was becoming a big boy:

"Hi there young man!"

"Hi there...!"

"How are you today?"

"I'm fine thank you!"

"Ah...that's nice! What a handsome young boy!"

"Thank you, ma'am...!"

V-II

Childhood learning experiences of the kind which I have gained are nearly impossible to lose. And when they are positive experiences, there is no desire to let them go. I believe that I conducted myself well enough to meet my parents' expectations. Those are also fond memories for me. I value and treasure them the way that I would value a chest of precious gems. For this, I am grateful to my parents.

Certainly I am not the only person to have had a good and loving upbringing. Most Americans will make a similar claim. There was actually a time in my life when I believed that all Americans would make a similar claim. It is the reason why today I kick myself for not knowing any differently. As hard as I may try, I cannot help thinking that some of us have memories we would rather forget. If I could do that, it would help me avoid the facts of what brought most of these men to the shelter. Yet I cannot avoid dwelling on the issue. If I only could, I might evade the negativity which is nearly about to consume me.

Existentialist writers of the early to mid twentieth century, penned names for some social conditions. One of the conditions was named 'nihilism'. It is a very complex condition to bring to light. When applied to the societies of mid century Germany, it could mean something quite different than when applied to our present day societies. Nothing however, can change its intent. It points to negative self awareness as a major contributor to social self destruction.

I have to be careful at this place to not allow myself to become too familiar.

If I do, we may find out exactly how negative things can get.

It has taken me two months to pay off the bills which got me thrown out of my apartment. I figure another two or three months are all that I need to work my way out of here! I am one of those residents who pay a daily fee. I have to practice greater discipline in order for things to go right.

For the first time in my life, there is a need to ignore the people in front of me. The only instance where there was any compassion was the time when I heard that Jean left. He had requested, and was granted a bus ticket to 'up north'. I was not really sure he was gone until I saw the empty bunk where he slept. I was glad for him though. I hoped that in his old age, he would find a better and more permanent home.

The absence of feelings here can be explained. In fact, it touches on the definition of nihilism. No matter how I am approached, I can look them in the eye and believe that no one is there.

V-III

Living in a dormitory setting has given me a sense of urgency. I am beginning to care more about the direction in which my life is heading. For sure, I am not prepared to cast my lot with the brethren here. I am more focused on what I have to do in order to remain above them. I am of the mindset that my wants and needs are at the center of the universe. What I know of my personal being is contrary to what some here would have me believe.

It is impossible that I would sit around the buildings all day. Moping around aimlessly, pretending to be injured is not an option. Counselors would sometimes ask if I am comfortable going out to work in the extreme heat. I would tell them yes! They would ask if I needed assistance with my car fares. I would tell them no!

As far as I was concerned, I only needed a place to lay my head. Their rules and concerns were none of mine. That is of course, unless they worked against me. I ran into a situation in the dining room where we had gotten our signals crossed. Breakfast line started up at seven A.M. and was over at eight thirty. If someone had to go out before seven, they would not be served. My issue was that breakfast hours only benefitted those residents who did not leave early for work. And since everyone there was catching on with work crews, it only served those men who did not go out at all.

My complaint was taken up at a subsequent meeting, and the rules were amended to accommodate everyone. A resident manager would open the kitchen every morning at five. We could then have access to coffee, toast, and dried cereal. This arrangement was nothing like breakfast hour; but, it was better than going to work on an empty stomach.

On those rare days when I could find nothing at the labor centers, I made my way back to the shelter before breakfast was over. I gorged myself with eggs, bacon, sausage, grits, milk, and whatever else the resident cooks had to work with.

On most days I would walk to the nearest labor finders. Mine was about two miles from the yard. I always tried to be among the first ten names on the list; it would assure me of being sent out. After a month or so my popularity with labor finder's clients was beginning to soar. The placement bosses were sending me to work on sites that were at the top of their 'must-do-well' list. I was proving my worth on jobs such as the difficult construction cleanup. This work requires vey little mental effort. You only need to stay on task, have good judgment, and good physical strength. Most construction sites were getting to look similar, if not the same. The job itself was to remove all discarded materials left at the nearly completed site.

I would be taken there by eight in the mornings. Sometimes I was alone, sometimes with a co-worker, sometimes with a team. We made a quick assessment of the site. Then we decided on how much time and difficulty it would take. We worked at the rate of speed that was determined by how much time it would take to clean up. We never sold ourselves short by finishing in less than eight hours.

The discarded materials were usually large beams and planks, scrap iron, sawdust, and fitted tiles. We spent our day collecting the stuff, and tossing it into open-ended dumpsters.

Landscaping sites were a little bit easier. Those would involve placing squares of sod-grass on the ground. But our rule is, 'until you arrive at a work site don't presume to know what you may end up doing'. At a development in an outlying county, one day I learned that I have a natural talent for grading dirt. The houses in the community had large front and back yards. The drainage systems were nicely planned. Most yards however, were still a huge mound of dirt. We were left with the job of leveling them out. There were some women on this crew. They were given sod-grass. The men grabbed up shovels and wheel barrows. I ended up with a rake. The landscaper on site described to me how the dirt had to be graded. Then he left in his truck.

The houses on our block had a stream that ran along the back yards, which separated them from a golf course. The men began to spread dirt at a rapid pace. The girls stood by with fresh sod, waiting for me to level the dirt. It appears simple enough to the untrained eye. The problem though, lies in finishing the entire yard in the correct grading. The sewers in front of the house, along with the stream around back, provide excellent drainage. But that system is useless if rainwater is allowed to settle on the grass. My task as I saw it was to facilitate run-off.

Where some yards made a simple slope, the ones I graded had a complex set of grooves and curves, more pleasing to the eye. I took into account, the relationships between patios and rear walls. I allowed some level areas for playground equipment and the like. Additionally, more pits and fewer slopes would prevent balls, as well as small children from tumbling into the stream.

There was no foreman. We just helped each other out and labored as hard as we could for eight hours. I had become one of the guys by now. At this level, each worker knows what the other person is capable of doing. Any action that drew positive reactions was used over and over, to the crew's advantage. Things didn't always go smoothly but we tried. The women contributed their best as well. Karen is known to everyone at the center as a good worker; even though as a female, she has issues of strength. She has helped to establish guidelines for women such as no furniture moving sites, no palette stacking, no one person sites, and no after-parties!

On this day she had become curious as to whether or not she could grade yards as effectively as I had been doing. As the conversations leaned towards her points of view, I still had my doubts. She appeared fully capable when I handed the rake to her. But as Baron stated, this was not a good time to experiment. He and Karen have been regulars at the center for more than five years. They agreed that our work was going smoothly and looking good. That was the bottom line. Our objective at all sites is to get called back. After a few strokes she gave the rake back to me. The crew let out a small cheer. Karen and I shook hands and we moved on to the next house.

That entire summer, my mind was on keeping my work together, as I worked on keeping my mind together. My thoughts never ventured beyond the task at hand. My mind never drifted, the way it habitually has done. If one were to say that I was on a mission, I would not disagree.

V-IV

In the process of being sensible, we put together a daily quota of thoughts. We conjure up solutions to problems that on other days would not be problems at all. We make issues on the grounds of baseless devices that can be quashed at the drop of a pin. Being reasonable is the act of giving oneself up to the notions of facing the day ahead

So we work, we chat, we laugh, and we try to stay abreast of the latest news. We turn our minds to more cosmopolitan things. Entrenching ourselves as we go, in business, church, sports, night clubbing, and so forth. Stones are left unturned because they needn't be disturbed. We can see where our lives are going at a glance. We accept things as they are because our environment has been made whole for us.

When someone plans his daily agenda, he must use logic. Things which he plans to do must coincide perfectly with things which he knows will be in effect. To have an agenda for the week, he must be reasonably sure that step five will be as certain to happen as step one. He can be comfortable in assuming that his status quo will not change by the end of the week.

As a result, his patterns become guidelines. Acceptable behavior as such, becomes routine behavior. And try as we may to avoid it, our behavior becomes predictable.

Nobody wants to see his wheels spinning in a rut. So we come up with new topics of conversation. And we find new ways to entertain ourselves. Knowing that all things change, we spend our days in virtual order. One day our worlds will implode with new technology and mechanisms. But today, we only want to be in our favorite shells.

Sometimes a person will have an idea that looks farther down the road. That person sees something new in what has become of our daily lives, our daily agendas, and of the here and now. Will it involve catastrophic changes along the lines of Hurricane Katrina? Or will there be small undercurrents of change, as in a charismatic new personality?

Ideating takes a lot of time. It detracts from what we have already planned to do. For some however, it's no waste of time. At every turn, someone is on the lookout; asserting new values, and extolling new ways. We cannot allow our rituals to go stale. When we do, someone will likely reinvent the automobile; causing us to go faster, have shorter patience, and get away for a few more days. Or someone will reinvent movie cameras; so that we don't have to wait for the traveling show, wonder about a beautiful starlet, or dream about adventure.

Then again, sometimes we plot to divert the inevitable. We build sea walls to keep the ocean in check. We build Great Walls to keep away the enemy. We make treaties to avoid conflict. And because conflict means change, sometimes we honor those treaties to stay at impasse.

To resist change is a greater challenge than to create progress. It is part of human nature to be inventive. We might stumble onto new ways of doing things quite unexpectedly. We find that by slightly altering an old formula, a new acceptable system has been created. On the other hand we can progress by trial and error. By using several different techniques, we plod and plunder until we arrive at the purported results. Sometimes we depend on science. Experimentation and methodology is an age-old practice. Often functional; often a comedy of errors, it is relied upon immensely. Still, science with all its mysteries remains at odds with other traditional practices.

Moral and religious dogma place their scrutiny upon all new technology. Yet today's societies would have grown very little without it. For modern continental societies which have found themselves advanced by leaps and bounds, the choice is obvious: either let nature take her course and stay with her natural pace, or continue to disturb her balance until our rustic globe is no more.

Stemming the tides of progress is a difficult job. Only in recent decades have we considered the harm being done in the name of progress. We have been defying nature's reign. We attack her with pollution of rivers, toxic waste, acid rain, non-biodegradable pesticides, nuclear testing, and global warming to name a few. Our political leaders can be heard trying to deny these effects; all in the name of progress.

The greatest progress now that our society can make is to slow down the urge to make more progress. Our greatest flaw is that we want to stare contemptuously at other non-progressed societies. Almost any society other than our own modern one falls into the category of 'lesser'. They include pre-literate historical, arctic societies, jungle bourn clans, ethnic traditional, desert tribes, rural societies, and third-world nations among others.

It gives us pleasure to look down our noses at those groups. To change this instinctive side would be beneath us. We arduously desire this privilege: a privilege which we manifested upon ourselves; yet one which we pursue in peril. We choose to look for scientific answers to our problems. That would be the progressive way to deal with them. We would use the scientific method to undo problems with the scientific method! We would ignore the wisdom of early Greek philosophers who told us to take the middle path. They believed that all things should be done in moderation. They advised 'nothing in excess'.

For those of us who believe that we should never look back, our planet issues a crystal clear warning. It is that, the earth can adjust itself to changes in atmospheric status. If we remain constant at our modern rate of depletion however, there will be no turning back. The central question for us is... "does man have the ability to confront his passion for progress?" Can we look to the future with an eye towards lessons learned from the past? I believe those lessons are pertinent, and that we can.

Tomorrow when we draw up our next agendas let us show regard for natural law. Many of us just want to be left to our devices: free to roam and rove; left alone with our friends. We are not willing to change our ways in order to affect a greater need. Though it may be an urgent need, we are not motivated to seek any other course.

Why shouldn't we look to the not-so-distant past? Look to those times when man was less of a threat to himself? Why shouldn't we look at times when the work was harder, the aim was clearer, the effort was more sincere, and the results were more pleasing?

We consider ourselves more civilized than our forefathers because we have invented ways to circumvent hard work. Let us consider for an instant that hard work is the backbone of all great civilizations.

Rather than stand in reverence of the Great Pyramids of ancient times, our scientists dig into them. They uproot and dismantle them. When in reality, the only mystery therein is how we lost the ancient work ethic. There are far more examples of hard work done by the ancients than can be set upon these pages.

The likelihood is that ancient builders were in awe of their own results. For millenia, their approach to daily life has stood as proof of man's superiority to other species. Modern man is apt to prove his superiority to nature herself. But what is it in the nature of man that will send his quest awry?

For certain, it is a flaw that we call 'vanity'. Nowadays we can go almost anywhere without ever taking a step. We could potentially at the flip of a switch, destroy every living organism. We satisfy all of our intellectual needs on the computer. We search for a nicer wardrobe, a more stylized car, or perhaps a form letter to explain why we can't be at work.

We are intelligent enough to know that we cannot contaminate the air we breathe. The logical next step would be to disallow contaminants. We can slow down our need for mechanical energy. That way, we might avoid raising the ante on pollutants. As we gamble more and more with forces that have yet to be understood, we come closer and closer to exposing ourselves to divine judgement. When it comes time to show our true nature, will we have what it takes? Have we allowed our love affair with science to create this modern lazy fare? And worst of all! Have we lost the common bonds that tie generations to generations: the generations of mankind?

VI-I

I have become comfortable with my new stability at the shelter. I would not define it as a comfort zone; rather, a zone of being at rest. I underwent a major transition with my core family. As one of the youngest of seven brothers I have always been on the receiving end of orders. Especially so when my oldest brother is twenty five years older than I. There are actually nephews and nieces who are older. I became guardian of my parents' well- being; and as such, was proven also to be the guardian of our family values.

I was able to move back in with my parents when no one else could. My decisions were the ones that carried the most weight. Only I was directly involved with day-to-day situations. It is true that I benefitted from financial contributions of my siblings, and I continued to look up to them. But it is also true that no one else was able to recourse and return home the way that I had done. The feel-good question of the decade has been "How are mom and dad?"

A conceptualized comfort zone which I had worked towards all of my life has just not fallen into place; though for some inexplicable reason I feel at best eased about myself. It is the kind of feeling that teenaged volunteers at the shelter must get when I allow them to do my chores. They helped!

As to their real functions here I cannot say! I 'will' say that they are kind, wide-eyed and generous. They are members of youth groups that have travelled from various parts of the country. I admit to sharing more unity with the group from New York, though they are all nice kids.

I must seem a curiosity to them because I am always at work. I return to the shelter around dinner time and hit the showers. I am usually among the last to finish eating, and I help out in the kitchen and dinning room. I don't know exactly how these kids interpret my presence here but I'm sure they know that I don't require their condescendence.

Nevertheless, they are very kind and eager. I respect youth who work on developing stronger qualities. I respect also their desire to learn about aspects of society that are different from their own. That is why I agreed to participate when counselors asked me to address some youths at a speak- around.

We had a gentleman who spoke on the subject of how alcoholism had confounded his life. Then another gentleman spoke about his war with drugs and the police. When I spoke they were surprised to hear about my college degrees and about the certifications which I hold. They nodded in agreement that I more than likely would move beyond this current phase. And they applauded my durability. Most importantly, they identified with my struggles, and recognized that it's a thin line which separates one station in life from another.

As far as my current pursuits, there is no experience needed. I work at the time and at the stride which fate has chosen for me. When all is said and done, I only hope that I have worked hard enough. It is not yet time to stand back and admire what I have done. There are highways yet to be travelled.

The blurry lines which stood before me are becoming more defined. I have begun to formulate patterns of behavior, and ways of coping with this environment. For example, I will take off one day of the week and go to some cross-town motel. I stay there all day relaxing, and clearing my thoughts. By ten o'clock at night I am back at the dormitory for roll-call. This is one way of separating myself from the realities of a term that I don't want to hear; that crazy word 'homeless'.

I have other options. I have a cousin and a brother in the area with whom I communicate from time to time. There are also associates who are not averse to having a roommate. But, in all honesty I have been struggling with issues of being intolerant. My abruptness with friends in recent months has left me on the outside. I have been desiring space, and requiring only short term relationships. I am still trying to reconcile the causes of my recent attitudes. Yet I can say for certain that I have not offended anyone.

I keep my walkman radio on my person. I get the best reception when I am at a park across the street. So that's where I can be found in my spare time. Other residents know better than to disturb me unless they have something constructive to say. Their issues of... "do you have a dollar?"... "Can I get a cigarette?" or ... "Where is your other radio?" have all grown tired! I'm better now at refusing people. I have learned to ignore them without feeling guilty about it. I'm still a nice guy. But I have lost all signs of being naïve.

Even members of the youth groups are reluctant at times to approach me. It could be that they respect my distance. I am trying not to be unpleasant; so, often I will speak when I am spoken to.

However, they have a goldmine in Mr. Long. These groups are church based. They do not impose religion upon us, but they are drawn to Mr. Long's incessant spouting about the bible. He is a talkative, graying man who always boasts about the cars and homes that he once owned. He says he lost everything because he was living in sin. He claims now to have discovered God, and is working towards turning is life around. His familiarity with bible scripture however leads me to believe otherwise. He has a bible that was given to him, but he apparently already knows what's in it. He finds a different suit of clothes every week to wear to church on Sundays. Strangely though, neither he nor anyone else can properly fix a necktie. I've done it for him the last couple of weeks because he remains unable to do so himself. On the other hand he walks around the buildings asking for help with his necktie. It just might be an excuse to show everyone his new suits.

When talking to the visiting kids, Mr. Long always strikes a chord. He embellishes his conversations with parables relating to 'what the lord said'. One day as I walked onto the patio there was a group of about twenty kids there. They seemed to be in a very spiritual way with their yells of "'amen", and "that's right" and so on. At the center of the group I saw Mr. Long. I paused for a moment to get a line on what was happening. Quoth Mr. Long! "...and the lord said unto Zophar, I will exacteth from thee only that which thine eniquity deserveth!" Then came a thunderous roar and applause. I smiled and eased my way past.

Since that time, I've had some dubious thoughts about the responses of those teenagers. I have become cynical during these past few months and have been attributing cynical motives to people who may well not be. Consequently, I am wondering if those kids were enraptured by the lessons of his sermon, or by the man himself. I wonder if they were applauding, not what the lord said, but the eloquence and force of a man who for some years now has been labeled 'homeless'.

Mr. Long shows off the new suit that he will be wearing to church.

My father also loved to pray. He would say grace before meals. And when I was very young we would say prayers at night. His most sincere payers were always said on the nights before we left home to go visit my grandmother. It always gave us a feeling of security. We felt safer, having asked to be in god's hands.

When I began making the journey to stay with my grandparents for the summer, I was about six years old. Before we took to the interstate my family would get together and pray for a safe trip to New York, and a safe summer for me. Although I did a lot of new things over the summer, my father had already guaranteed me that I would be safe. I had no choice but to believe him. It occurs to me now that the youth groups are under the same protector. For that reason, I respect their love for Mr. Long.

Upon my arrivals in New York, we had no specific aims or directives. I was learning gradually to live the way my extended family did. In the mornings, my cousin Willie and I would go to the playgrounds for some handball and dodgeball. After that we went home for lunch. After lunch we would go skateboarding. In the evenings, we roamed and played with other youngsters in the neighborhood until nightfall. Sometimes my father would call to check on me. I could tell when he was on the phone because my grandmother talked with him in the same loud voice that he used to speak with her. It was as if, a long-distance talk on the phone was the same as a long-distance talk down the street. Nevertheless, without the frequent calls, I would become homesick. As much fun as I had with my relatives, it was still difficult being away from my family.

Granny did everything right according to my parents. She was guiding me through my young days the way she had raised my father. It occurred to me that almost nothing had changed for her. Uncle Jim was still living with her, and she still got financial assistance from the government. From time to time she would even refer to me by my father's name. I still remember with fondness how she called out to me one day, "Okay Stevie, time to watch 'The Price Is Right'!" I laughed and said "Alright granny, I'll change the T.V. station if you call me Al."

For all intentions I was my father re-created. In those days I couldn't say if I were a Georgian or a New Yorker. In other words, there would be a large gap between myself; and a southern boy visiting here for the first time. There were some cultural differences in my summer home-life. Grandmother liked to drink a glass of wine. There was no drinking in my parents' house. Uncle Jim was always out drinking, nightclubbing, and playing the numbers. I never knew my father to incorporate those vices into his lifestyle. And I heard from others that Jim was on good behavior during my stays. They said that he was only respecting my father's wishes. The two were very close. I've seen them sitting and talking for hours. But they were very different. Jim never had a family, and he was always smoking 'Luckies'.

Next thing I know; I'm in Rosie's arms. Rosie is my other grandmother. Dad once told me that her family was from another country, but I loved being with her as much as with his mother. Rosie still lived with my great-grandmother. Being here was a different story altogether. They were a very proud group. We communicated very well. When people saw us they knew that we were family. Rosie always planned ahead. She would tell me step by step what we were going to do in the upcoming week. She would take time off from her vegetable store. We played board games, tested my skills on the same piano where my mother learned to play, and then we would visit my aunts and more cousins.

Whenever we watched television, she always sat with her arms around me. She was constantly explaining what the stories were, and what was going to happen. One day I said to her, "Rosie be quiet, let me enjoy the story!" She laughed into hysteria. Then she kissed me on the cheek and said "Okay darlin'!"

The aunts that I know of, all worked in Rosie's store. They always wanted to know how things operated down south. And they would also quiz me about uncle Jim.

I was a pseudo-ambassador between the two groups. A sort of unwitting agent of kinship; I kept everybody on the same page. I don't ever recall seeing them together. But my grannies often communicated by phone when I was around. I would sometimes overhear them plotting a timetable. How long will I be here? When will I be there? Who's going to have me wherever? It stopped just short of being antagonistic.

Those were points in my life which by themselves are enough to sustain my positive outlook. Knowing where I come from, and how much love there is, how could I ever encounter a period of self-doubt?

VII-II

What could have transpired in my world to make me think of myself as counter productive? This mode of thinking is in itself, a kind of nihilism. It is a retraction of the person who came into being, all those years ago. It is an impediment to those traits which I have exhibited, and am expected to exhibit at all times.

At the same time I must realize that I am not the same person I have always been. Though I have always defied being categorized, there are circumstances which cannot be overlooked. Where I once held a middle-class job and earned a middle-class income, I now do menial labor for minimum wages. Where I once lived in a very nice apartment with all the amenities of 'the good life', I now live in a homeless shelter. Have I in this short time become so altered of mental and emotional strength as to affect my basic instincts? I think not. I have to conclude that there's more to this kind of lifestyle which is inherently contradictory to me. It's not just the matter of being here. That I can do! It is the predominant outlook on life, of which I have to stay cognizant.

I think that the counter productiveness takes hold when any person, or any aspect of this place shows the potential of making me belong. If I let them, they would portray me as a practicing member of the society of the homeless. I admit that I needed the time away from it all which I have consumed so far. As much, I would say as I needed the distraction. I have yet to see the face of an all-new world as it is spinning its way towards me. At this point all is not clear. The lessons I am learning are pertinent only to my immediate survival. Nothing I'm absorbing here offer's any clue to the bigger picture.

The big picture is more than likely tied in to the evolving face of my core family: an evolution which has yet to come full circle.

I have refused to take part in the qualms of my family when my own thoughts and my own life are still in disarray. I also refuse to placate the aims of my brethren at the shelter. To state it mildly, their agendas are different from mine.

The more that I communicate, the more I find out about what goes on. A resident jokingly asked me one day if I was going to take my paycheck and spend it across town. I told him..."Not this week!" I was saving up for a dental appointment. I told him that I had a toothache, and left it at that. Later that day I was told to go to the clinic. They looked in my mouth, and told me that I was going with the dental program. It consists of a list of dentists who volunteer their time and expertise to assist the needy. At first I refused to take part. But the money I earned was too little to pay for what I needed to be done. Someone told the nurse that I was having toothaches and would not go to the program. So she came to me. She explained that the program was for everyone who qualified. She pointed out that I was no exception, and that it would serve no purpose to not take advantage.

A week later I was in a van with ten other patients, on the way to the dentist. My pain problem was solved and I was greatly relieved. I had an unshakable urge nevertheless to pay the man for his services: though no such payment was required.

The following day I went to work with my face swollen. When I returned I saw the other patients sitting on the patio moaning and groaning in pain. The hot topic was pain pills. They all wanted to know what I got, so I told them. Nothing! The only medication I required was aspirin! Again, I had set myself up to be laughed at. Only this time it was more like ridicule. It was as if they wanted to say to me, "You idiot."

For my purposes though, I had once again set myself apart from their motives. And again, unfortunately this is creating self doubt. I would never consider myself as being better than they. I would only consider that I could not find comfort living in society's underbelly.

Consequently, even this tone lends itself to the prevailing element; that is, denial. Denial of any associative properties: denial which of itself, is not good.

The effectiveness with which I conduct my daily affairs, ultimately cannot be good for the other residents. I am proving myself to be intractable. My example is one which the counselors favor. I have given them some small reason perhaps to consider why the others cannot be like me. Yet I know in my heart of hearts, that this is not what I set out to do! Yes, I am doing what I have to do to re-establish myself. But as an example of the others, this cannot be good.

I saw an old friend, Bennie eating in the dining room. He explained to me that he had just finished six moths in jail, and was in the "Half Way" program. For him, this place is one of very few alternatives. It would be a shame if this opportunity did not exist. It is apparent that the facility here with all its programs evolved over the years to meet the needs of such a person as Bennie.

Fishman is in a losing battle with a rare form of arthritis. For weeks on end he can be as well and as healthy as anyone. Then without warning he will collapse in agonizing pain. A rescue ambulance picked him up one morning and took him to the hospital. Fish was completely immobilized by the attack. I am not sure about the specifics of his treatment. I know that he must always go to an emergency room.

No employer would risk hiring him. Subsequently, he cannot cover his frequent hospital visits with any kind of worker's insurance. His one and only hope is the program available to him at the shelter.

The list of related examples goes on and on. This shelter is a well run institution and an absolute necessity. Had I not encountered it for myself, I might have gone through life with some typical concepts. I have always imagined this place to be the center of the universe for ne'er-do-wells. To learn a different aspect can only be good for me.

I have also found tendencies that should be placed at another end of the spectrum. There are many who fall into the category of chronic abusers. The problem is that almost anyone can get a bed. This is why the shelter is perpetually at capacity. The fee for a week is the equivalent of one day's pay. Most of those who are turned away are persons who could not get past the drug screen. It is the reality for the vast majority. Despite the philanthropy, the reform, and the humanitarian aide, most residents are habitual returnees: men who have played out their options on the streets, then returned to the shelters when the world got cold.

Because I have such a determination to meet my own needs, I am resistant to the in-house support systems. They are intended for my well-being. Everyone is convinced that I should partake of their availability. Yet, I tend to make my way around those services. The fact of the matter is that I have never known, nor have I ever expected those services to be free-of-charge.

My concern now is that the persons who provide those services might begin to reconsider their importance. It is counter productive of me to imply even slightly that they are not necessary. I am seeing the dichotomy now at every turn. It is causing me to think about what productivity really is.

VII-III

The longer I dally at this phase, the more I am sure of how aimless it is. The longer I pursue this morose mission, the more clearly I see the hopelessness of it all. We know that the rich inevitably get richer. And because our modern world is getting smaller, we also know that the poor are getting railroaded. To avoid this possibility I recognize that I must not thrive in this underclass. It is a trap.

Life in the privileged classes is congested. A growing population has turned this system of Capitalism into the "haves" and the "haves not". The "haves not" are being swept into a corner. We stroll right by them every day. We see a man feverishly twisting, then combing through his hair with dirty fingers. But what can we do about it? From where I sit! Nothing!

And what about myself; why have I been pressed into the roll of Prometheus? Will it be possible to redeem myself from a life of brainless labor? Like the Ancient Greek citizen, my sentence is to to push a giant boulder to the top of a steep hill. It is possible to survive a life in which hard labor is all that is done. I see others do it every day. Although a different way for me, it is still an aspect of the world at-large.

I can go on this way for as long as my strength lasts. As long as I am motivated to persevere, I can stand up to any test put before me. To say that I am the maker of my own destiny, is to presume that I am on a good path in my life. But to assume that I would not be touched by these surroundings would be another step in denial. After all, a missionary who does not get the fever has not really been in touch with the tribesmen.

Though I remain aloof; I will not deny these simple connections. The cure for any symptoms I may contract is still self determination and hard work. I know the pitfalls of slothfulness. I have seen with my own eyes, men and women who allowed the world to float by them without having moved a muscle. I have seen blameless winos lying in the gutter crying…"I want a brew…I want a brew!"

As I did on that occasion, and as I have done on all other occasions, I just ignored their cries. I learned as a child that it is a simple matter to separate oneself from the sins of others. This is particularly so when those others have fallen to such a disgraceful level. My parents set a very different example for me.

I remember a time at home when business was slow and things were not up to par. But those times were few and far between. My childhood image of my father is one of a strong proud man. Sometimes he would walk to his shop. When he returned home in the evenings, we kept watch to see him turn the corner; his wide-brimmed hat shielded the sun from his eyes. His broad steps gave no indication of having put in a ten hour day. And his broad smile betrayed the stern tones of the night before. The cinnamon buns and sodas that he brought never hurt his popularity.

Sometimes when he drove the car to work, he would take us for a drive afterward. We used to go to the stores and then sightseeing around the city. Then we would go to the country to get some artesian well water. Our family dog was named Bullet. I think he was given that name because of his ability to chase after our car. He could run for long distances before tiring out and giving up. He was my favorite pet ever. He got the same love and care as everyone else. Those days were so long, and filled with so much fun that it is difficult for me to conceive of any family with a different lifestyle.

Too bad for us now our friend Bullet is gone; he represents a link between myself and siblings in my age group. Only we can discuss with familiarity, those times and his antics. And in a broader sense, Bullet represents another family quality. When I recall seeing that orange colored dog through the rear window; how he kept pace with us for miles; is durability; his desire, I can't help seeing the indefatigable heart that beats within us. One family, one group, one chance to make a statement in life: this is what my friend Bullet represents. This is the example which I must set.

VIII-I

For people in today's society, the most important thing in life is making money. Approximately three decades ago, America went off the 'Gold Standard' for economic parity. That term was once well-known around the world. Subsequently, precious gold extracted from the earth was not plentiful enough to satisfy man's lust for wealth. Because it is a finite source, gold could not hold up to financial speculation. It was written off for a more abstract base: a formless, shapeless system of gain. Personal wealth has the ability to soar now to infinity. It will be mitigated only by how far one's calculator can tally; whether it is backed by gold or not.

In summary, we have outgrown another of the earth's natural resources. More significantly, we have severed our ties with an age-old tradition. We broke apart a measuring stick that motivated kings and nations to plunder the world. From the Conquistadores of Spain to the Boors of Africa, from the Pharaohs of Egypt to the Forty-Niners of California, and from the Aztecs of Mexico to Nazi Germany; now finally we are free to speculate beyond our earthly supplies.

Most significantly of all, the change inferred that our leaders are wise enough to control such an abstract system. Up to now we have not put into place a system of laws that defines how we mete out monetary wealth. Our economic system has to operate on the assumption that there is a limit to individual wealth. We will have to redefine the term rich. We must cautiously enter our new definition. It must at least mirror the traditional one. Someday someone will amass computerized wealth that cannot be brought to an end.

Are we better for having written off our earthy crown? Or have we doomed ourselves to patriotic paper bills; valueless script; wallets full of plastic that can be written off before it can be spent? Where do our investing skills go from here?

With each new day, we loosen the ties that bind us to the earth, our history, and to our basic instincts. It was necessary to abandon the gold-for-script equation in order to enhance personal wealth. Therefore it will be necessary to be loyal to a system of abstract values.

But what part of our culture is being poised to obtain this wealth? I would say that the "haves" have made life a bit more uncertain for the "haves not".

Wealth is a function of the "haves". Whatever major changes happen, take place without the participation of the "haves not".

VIII-II

Let us consider an hypothetical situation. Let us say that ten students are about to graduate from a prestigious business school. They are about to receive post graduate degrees in computer technology. They are ranked as the top ten students in their class. At some point in the school year they come together and agree to form a business partnership. They postulate that as a team they could not miss being successful. They believed that whatever the venture, their cartel would be among the best in the nation. They could apply their talents to any client they felt would benefit from their well learned services.

Each student had proven that he has the ability to excel. Their professors had given them a green light to pursue whatever end they believed possible. University insiders attest to the genius of their group. The students have so much confidence in themselves that they set out immediately to establish a corporation. The top student, whom we shall call Maggie was selected as president. The students with the next highest grade points, Sumie and Cumie became executive vice-presidents. Each was given two executive assistants. The student who followed those seven in grade point was named chief executive officer of the company. The two remaining were named his assistants. They combined to make a formidable resume'. Inexperienced as they may have been, they were the envy of many in the business community.

They drew up rules and agreed to the chain of command. They defined roles and drew up contracts for each member; to be notarized and endorsed contractually. They committed themselves to the cartel before they set out in business.

Being green to the world of business, they had no useable references. Their most usable senses came from the textbooks and courses which they had mastered. They needed to translate that scholarship to the real world.

The one course which they had in common was computer programming. All of their subsequent meetings would become seminars related to that topic. They finally decided that cartel possessed an unrivalled expertise in computer programming. They agreed to form their company in that field.

They easily obtained small business loans from the government. They used the money to establish business offices that matched a high profile. They moved into a building that drew raves from the community. It was a gleaming edifice of modern architecture with room for expansion. It was a seven story wonder. Maggie's office took up most of the top floor. There would be enough remaining space for the various aides, secretaries, and pages which she will need. Sumie and Cumie had their offices on the floor below. Beneath them were the vice presidents' assistants and the company board room. The board room will become strategic as a meeting place for many important functions.

Although cartel had no real experience in community services, they were already being visited by high profile clients looking to get an edge. They held the promise of becoming one of the nation's top programming firms. Their skills had been put in portfolios for any potential client to see. Their reputation as the number one up and coming business firm in the nation was an unexpected 'plus'. Cartel was able to present their new services to high profiled clients who waited with opened arms.

With the question of their marketability resolved, they were ready for the next bold step. In order to assess the purchasing power of their company, cartel hired an economic advisory firm. They had not completed a business transaction as of yet, but had compiled a long list of clients. Their services would begin at the start of the new fiscal year. Based on those events, their company was given a net investment worth of one hundred million dollars. It was astounding news for them. When they posted those figures on the stock market boards, their purchasing powers increased by tenfold.

Prestige began to soar. Maggie was able to visit important businessmen in her own private jet. Their lifestyles were verification of the wealth at their command. By the time cartel decided to close the list of jobs for the year, their net worth had made another quantum leap.

It was time to face the world. They spent the next few weeks buying office equipment. They opened their personnel center, and began hiring skilled staff. They became fully functional. The operation was a go!

With a few days remaining before their services went on line, the cartel hired a brokerage firm. They had opted to sell stock in the company at the request of an outside investor. This move proved to be another windfall. Overnight they became a "Fortune 500" company. Their prestige was growing world wide. Speculators began investing wildly, snapping up any available stock in the company. Some paid five times the posted value, just to be in on the ground floor. Now, there was only one day left before they opened their doors for business. The ten graduates held a meeting in the board room. They evaluated how far they had come, and how much had changed. The most glaring change was their wealth. In their wildest dreams they had never imagined this would happen. Only five months earlier, they were wide-eyed college kids. On this day they are kings and queens. To no one's surprise they found themselves split evenly on a major issue.

On the one hand they worked on projects that lay on the table before them. On the other hand they discussed what to do with their new found wealth. By the end of the day it was apparent which side carried the most weight. Their famous new stature was taking a back seat to what they really are; kids just out of school. The scholarship and drive which pushed them to the heights of possibility was about to abandon them.

They laughed at each other, then gave a collective sigh of relief. They knew that Maggie had received another standard message at the end of the business day before. It was accepted procedure in stock circles. Every successful company is sent notification about any "buyout" offer.

At this moment they were contemplating the unthinkable. They wondered what they would see if they opened the buyout number.

Sumie closed his eyes, then clicked on the computer screen. Then, slowly parting his eyelids he peeked at the number. Then he said out loud…"six… point five…billion!" Then, collapsing to the floor he whispered…"dollars."

The youngsters sprang into a brainless dance. Some jumped on the tables, some crawled across the floor. They lost any semblance of professionalism. As Maggie tore off her name tag and hurled it across the room, Cumie dissolved the partnership with some final words: "How sweet this is!"

VIII-III

The above events are fictional and to the best of my knowledge, have never taken place. This situation is written as a parable. It is presented by this author to illustrate a moral. It puts emphasis on the pitfalls of greed. Greed is the expectation of amassing things in excess.

Furthermore, it addresses our system of speculation, which can lead to almost any outcome. The above mentioned students realized a pot of gold. They were able to obtain what everyone dreams of; wealth beyond belief. Their lives took a turn for the best yet they don't know what hit them.

They captured a prize that resulted from the pitfalls of speculation. Investors who will never know the whole story still pursue their dreams of financial gain. The investors and the students became part of a cycle which could find no boundary lines.

Most people in our times are driven by a desire to be wealthy. When the prize is an abstract golden egg, it is a difficult matter to liquidate. What are the ramifications; the legalities; the standards across the board? Who becomes the big winner? Who will be the losers? How many heads will roll?

Someone will find a way to get around all these questions. But one can only speculate. There is no speculation about motive however. Everyone desires to be rich. It seems nothing could have prevented what unfolded in this story. Very few legal restrictions are in place to guide these kinds of outcomes. Laws currently are such that the above mentioned monetary activity may actually happen.

Perhaps the lessons of our theoretical cartel will serve as a springboard for future legislation. A scenario such as this will require smarter lawmakers. This kind of activity on the part of the rich, will require laws that are more sensitive to effects on society at large. Better guidelines will take into consideration the other forces that are at work.

All governments have stratafications in class. Whether intentional or not, classes are generated by the societies they serve. The students in our parable are from an advantaged class. They were in a position of high status before they ever went to college.

They were heirs apparent to a capitalist society that perpetuated their success. The students could bank on their very high class education as well as some very high class cultural expectations. Those particular kids were products of an upper class environment. Their success was in fact the results of a controlled system. The same results are not available to graduates of a less prestigious institution. Our group of students were the prophesized benefactors. They were born with certain advantages, and followed through to fruition. All the forces of the well-to-do are at their disposal.

By no fault of their own, cartel perpetuated a middle class dream that is thousands of years old. The dream of boundless financial success has happened before and it will happen again. We as a society are powerless to prevent it. There will always be men and women who reap the potential rewards of conspired events. While most in society are reaching for the appearance of proprietary success, there will always be those in whose hands it actually resides.

Nevertheless, there are always peripheral forces at work. Unmitigated success for a small few in society will always generate those forces. By forces I mean those such as jealousy and envy: that is, when others desire to possess a similar status. They are forces which cannot be disregarded. They have proven to be glaring motives for rebellion. They led to the overthrow of the last Tsar of Russia. They led also to the beheading of the last King of France and his wife Marie Antoinette.

Our young capitalist society is not yet perfect. We have been trying throughout its brief history to divert those maddening forces. We say in our constitution that all men are created equal. But how many of us actually believe it? We have worked hard to put all citizens on equal footing. But this will never happen.

There will always be a spectrum of activity. A spectrum can diverge into many different directions. As a result, there will always be differences of opinion.

There will always be a range of success. As well, there will always be a range of failure. Consequently we must always be aware of a range of feeling which pervades our society.

In America, there are some who live in vaulted elation. They soar too high to require any advice. Still others live a middle class existence. They do nothing in excess. Then there are those who live in distress. Every day is another struggle.

Our society embraces a wide spectrum. We may someday live up to the Constitution's words. But it will come with much justification. We have to be perceptive enough to see what is happening on the periphery. There are men and women reaching out to us. Those in society who are not created equal will only know life at the bottom end of the spectrum. They are citizens who are in need of assistance.

IX-I

That summer between my fourth and fifth grades was a turning point
for me. It was the first time that I would be going with my parents to
visit relatives in Buffalo. The year before, I remained in down state
New York with my grandmother. And the year before that I stayed
in Georgia, with my father, while my sister and baby brother went to
Buffalo with my mother. That was a summer that did not go so well.
I don't know if it was because I had to stay home, or if it was because
my family was in half.

But that Buffalo summer was much nicer. I would be meeting even
more relatives, as well as seeing my cousin Helen again. Her family
had lived down south for many years before moving back to upstate.
She was one of my favorite playmates, and I had not seen her in nearly
three years.

IX-II

Along the way from down state to upstate, we made several planned stops. I was getting some ~~perspective~~ on how really big my extended family is. I was actually learning as we travelled. My parents tended to reminisce about those family members as we got closer to their residence. We were going steadily for Albany and dad's cousin Rudy on our first stop. The most memorable thing about him was how badly his breadth smelled. My father had us all roaring with laughter. When they were all still teenagers, he said, they decided to drive to Georgia. My father said they believed fumes from the muffler were getting into the car. He said they stopped to find the problem. Nothing seemed to help until they got into warmer weather, and were able to roll the windows down. My mother said that was when they realized that Rudy was the problem.

When at last we got to his house, Rudy was not what I expected. He was a pleasant man with a head full of long graying hair. He was soft spoken and neatly dressed. His wife had passed away and he was living with one of his sons and some grandchildren. As I recall, we stayed there one half day, and one night. My parents and he talked and joked about many things, but never once did the subject of his breadth come up. Rudy's son knew my older brothers, but he had never before met us. His kids were in the same grade at school as I. They were not very playful, because to this day I don't remember any of their names.

We left in the early morning. I remember Rudy waking me up to say goodbye and to give me a dollar. That was the one and only time I ever met him and his family. Timing was everything on the road, according to my father. To make the best way, leaving by sunrise was essential.

When I woke up later that morning, we were only a few hours outside Aunt Cora's. My father said that being a sleepyhead cost me a valuable lesson about highways. I would have to wait until next time to see how we go out of Albany, by driving southwest to the Pennsylvania line, then picking up the thru-way to Corning. It was important to him that I knew how to be in touch with our relatives. He did not use a map, nor did he ask directions. He knew the way from experience. He had travelled those roads many times.

When she took over the driving chores, my mother was not as adamant. Her only job was to give him a rest. She always watched him to be sure he wasn't getting sleepy. She liked to stop for an hour or so to eat and rest. I think she would have been very upset if she knew what dad and I did two summers prior. I didn't want to cause an argument so I didn't tell her that we drove straight through. After we had dropped her and the others off, we drove back to Georgia stopping only for gasoline. This is one characteristic that I can say positively I share with my father. When we were in travelling mode, our philosophy was 'gas and go'! Other than this, everyone says I look like my Grandma Rosie. Once dad and I decide upon a course of action, it is very difficult to repress. And by the way, he never got tired.

I must have dozed off again before we reached Aunt Cora's house, because I don't remember arriving there. What I clearly remember are the walls of bedrock that lined our highway. And I also remember a strange dream about driving to the top of the world:

ONE GREAT TOUR
I DREAM IN FANTASIES;
HOW THE ROAD LOVES ME:
SO PROUD OF HOW WE FARE;
HOW WE GET HERE TO THERE.

ALL I EVER DREAMED OF;
ALL THAT I EVER KNEW;
IS JUST THIS ONE GREAT
TOUR; ONLY THIS ONE
GREAT TOUR.

FEW THINGS CHANGE AS WE ROLL;
NEW TIRES GUARANTEED TO HOLD:
FIELDS OF CROPS LINE OUR WAY.
IT ONLY TAKES A DAY!

I CAN RELY ON YOU,
TO ALWAYS GET ME THROUGH!
ON THIS REALLY GREAT TOUR;
THIS IS JUST ONE GREAT TOUR.

And then I heard a woman's voice saying my name: Al...Al... it's me; it's your Aunt Cora.

It was a very soft wake up call. I took a couple of minutes to gather myself. "Oh! Aunt Cora! How are you doing?" I heard some applauding in the background. I turned around and saw some old familiar faces. "There's cousin Bill! What's hap'nin captain?"

And that's where my memories of what happened in Corning shifts gears. When I looked at my cousin Bill, I started to have some unwelcome images of the summer that Bill spent with us in Georgia. He is about four years older than I. The fact that he came to stay with us for the summer was not the problem. We were always back and fourth. I was five years old at the time. But even then, Aunt Cora's parting words sounded ominous. She said to my father; "Just remember that you are in charge!"

61

We would always hear little threats from dad. He would tell us that he was going to tan our hides, or whip our tails. But he never actually beat any of us. However, I remember the time when he paddled Bill real good! I look back on that incident and wonder how my father could have been so mean. But I realize now in my adulthood, that I also have never seen my father so angry. It makes me wonder now, just exactly what it was that Bill had done.

Nonetheless, Bill did not seem to hold a grudge. As long as I kept the two of them apart, everything was fine.

IX-III

I could not say for sure nowadays if we arrived in Buffalo by bus, train, boat or plane. All I can say is that we got there via route 80. We stayed for about a month. That was good planning because my mother was exhausted.

The entire summer is a blur. Some things though, stick out in my mind. First of all, I was amazed that we had to wear jackets in the evenings. I had known summer to be a time for short pants and T-shirts. Sometimes, we wore no shirts at all. Mom explained to me that the farther north you go, the colder the weather gets. That meant to me that Buffalo was north of every place else I had ever been. I was told by some more cousins that the wind blows off the Niagara Falls and whips through the streets like Mr. Jack Frost.

I am remembering a storefront. And I am remembering a church. It is quite possible that the two were one in the same. If my grandaunt were around today, I would ask her to be sure. I remember running the streets with Helen and some more kids. Even though she had changed, our friendship had not. When I first saw her in the apartment where they lived, she told me to have a "cheer". It sounded as though she forgot how to say the word "chair". I was sophisticated enough to not make an issue of it. Through my travels, dialect was one of the many things of which I had become cognizant. I recognized that she did not have the benefit of hearing various dialects. But seeing them again was good enough for me, so I accepted whatever she said.

It was a summer of high energy. There was a lot of running and jumping; and a lot of laughing and yelling. Our grandaunt took my mother and baby brother to see Niagara Falls. I remember being curious as to why I couldn't go. But at the end of the day, it was no big deal.

For some odd reason, a lot of feelings from that summer have stuck with me. Aside from the fact that my entire family was here, I cannot decipher any other reason for it. There is a possibility that my father was considering moving the family to here; but that was never discussed in my presence. Certainly, we did all the things that we did at home. We even had our own house.

I was amazed to learn that Canadian money is legal in Buffalo. To me, this was really impressive. Helen explained that it is legal because it is given out by the banks. So anytime that we went to the corner store we could use either American or Canadian coins.

By the summer's end I was a changed person. I had seen and done so many new things. I recall the difficult farewells when it was time to leave. There were tears and hugs. I remember taking part in the fondness. And I remember Helen saying "I love you."

From there, I barely remember anything else. Ensuing events are a blur. My family never made that drive again. We have exchanged post cards and phone calls, but that was the last time that I actually saw them. That summer, that great tour, and Helen, still reside in my heart.

After the journey, we were not as eager to hit the road. We did not have the urge to pack up and go as we so readily had done. Yes we were still on pace for the sixteen hour drive from Georgia To New York. But the journey to upstate had drained us all. We chalked it up to experience, and everyone was happy.

Moves like those are what made my core family, the centerpiece of my entire extended family. My parents must have realized at some point that we could not continue being all things to all people. So, without a significant reason to go there, that drive upstate is a needless trek. I'll just say that my siblings and I have another memory worth treasuring.

I really love all of my relatives. I have not had the opportunity to visit them again, though I thought as a child that I would. About that I am remorseful. One day if I am lucky, I will make that drive again.

X-I

The following summer, I was at my older brother's house in New Jersey. His wife Angie asked me where I learned to do word-find puzzles. "I help Ms. Cross; my teacher!" I replied. "I'm impressed." She smiled.

I was impressed with her as well. There they were: five years or so out of college, both in very fine professional careers, a young son, and living in the suburbs. They made quite an impression on me.

Before that summer I had seen my big brother Nate only three times. He and my two other big brothers were born before the Great War, and in the north. The other four of us are from a different era in my parents' lives, and born in the south. The eldest of my brothers, Andy, does not share the same mother as the rest of us. That fact has never detracted from his place in the family. As far as has been my experience, there has never been any type of displacement.

The coincidental separation of our family did not present a problem. We are family! And when we could, we got together. Nate and Syl had grown up, and moved back to the north before I was born. Andy never left New York. For my purposes, blood is blood, and my brother is my brother. As these two parts began to stabilize, our family became more of a unit. Visiting each other became easier to accomplish.

New experiences in my life have given me a new view of family structures. I was sitting one day on the patio at the shelter socializing with my old friend Bennie. He divulged to me that the only clothes he had been able to get since being released from jail were given to him by his brother's daddy. He lost me for a moment. Searching for a tactful response I asked him..."Do you and your brother have different fathers?"

It came out eventually that he has two brothers and one sister. All of whom have different fathers. Those revelations carried me to a brand new level of awareness. Keeping a tight lip, I passed it off as if it were not pertinent; as though what he told me were perfectly fine and normal. But I have trouble with any information that trips me up: even if only for a moment. I glanced at the situation in real time. I imagined that my father had six twin brothers, and that each one of my brothers could select one as a father. As such, my siblings were still my siblings, but each had his own father to help him out.

My normal thought patterns are calm and stoic. On that night they were stormy and crude. Why had no one told me before about this? How does it figure with the family life that I had known? Was I feeling insecure because I had just been kicked out of my traditional understandings?

I told myself that it shouldn't be bothering me at all. I know of many brothers and sisters who look completely different from each other. They play and work together. And they watch out for each other. That is the way it should be, and that is the way it is. The mother in Bennie's situation is the person who keeps the tradition of family going. Her genetics are what drives their hearts and keeps their bloodlines strong. Their independent purposes are what give them their individuality. Their unity is the source of their own family identity.

As different as it is, the family can never be put asunder. Before ritualism, comes family. Bennie's family life could easily parallel mine. It would take a lot more coordination and a lot more desire to function as a unit. The inherently disadvantageous elements of his family combine to make them weaker. Ultimately the decision rests with the parents. Because they caused the bloodlines to co-mingle, they bear responsibility for the outcome.

Who determined that Bennie's revelation is derogatory? To think that would be to think that his is the wrong kind of family. I will not be so quick to draw conclusions. Heaven forbid that I should give this family some issues of low self-esteem. Obviously, however, this unit is different. It lends itself to outside judging which more often than not, supplants any issues of high self-esteem.

X-II

My perspective has led me to conclude that this is one of society's flawed families. Each sibling is guided by a separate set of influences: each influence wrought with human feelings; each feeling spawned by a delicate chain of words.

Every child craves acceptance. It is the only way that he or she can thrive in the world. Being part of the basic family unit helps to insure that this person will survive pressure from the outside. Issues of love, companionship, and social development are major functions. When those functions are clear and satisfied, there is no reason why any child should be dismissed from connotations of a normal development.

One of the things that a child perceives is his station in society. He learns his status as a component of growing up. As are his parents' social functions, so are his. The child learns that he is a proud part of their social behavior. As his perceptions are in the early stages, all meanings are derived from and applied to the semantics of his parents. For purposes of his development, these perceptions are perhaps the best setting for a child. Since the child is a genetic offshoot of his parents he is probably similar to them in size, ability, nature, and resourcefulness.

By understanding the cultural status of his family and all its eccentricities, the child gets a head start on life. Although the child's status is determined by that of his parents', he is not bound by it. Today's children can make changes in how they were defined.

67

At an age when children begin to envision themselves in society, they are perfectly innocent. At a time when children are making vital decisions about their own abilities, they are also influenced by outside teachings. Their innate abilities help them to decide what course is best. Inner feelings get bared at every step of the way.

If a child perceives that certain social problems do not meet with his desires, his passive reactions become active. How the child reacts to those problems depends upon his own personal maturity.

Children in modern societies have common influences. As the world has grown smaller for adults, so it has for children. Foremost among which is early education. Children also are goaded with similar toys, clothes, and furniture. Other universal influences include music, movies, and television.

All these are proven quantities. They are generally accepted as proper and correct culture. Nevertheless, they have to be interpreted by each child in his own way. Not as much what to make of its significance, as how to play with it. The most well rounded children are ones who can make the pieces fit with the least amount of turbulence.

As we find on all scales of measure, there are peaks and there are valleys. We find some below average elements, some average, and some above average. Every once in a while there will be the exceptional. As it regards human ability, there will sometimes be an individual who defies the odds. An example of this is the barefoot Olympic runner Abebe Bekele. I have always been interested in anything having to do with sports. Every Olympic year brings an opportunity for me to watch the best athletes in the world compete for their countries. These men and women all fall into the category of exceptional. Bekele is an example of someone who had risen above all probable expectations.

It was difficult at first to figure out why he chose to run a marathon without shoes. A sports announcer pointed out that many Egyptian athletes were too poor to get standard training equipment. As a result, they practiced barefooted. What seemed very odd and painful to others was perfectly normal to this runner. Still it put him at a disadvantage. Every pavement pounding step had to be an agonizing one. I kept thinking about the pebbles, shards of glass, and small ridges under his feet. Yet nothing broke his stride.

Then I wondered what could motivate a labor so arduous as his. A sports announcer also made the point that if Mr. Bekele were to win this event, he could make more money than he could working an entire lifetime. I became an instant admirer.

I knew the odds were against him. I am a realist so I never let my hopes get too high. As long as he remained in he lead pack, I kept cheering for Mr. Bekele. I saw on that day that some people cannot be denied their aims. He entered the Olympic stadium ahead of the other world class competitors. Bekele ended up winning the race and the hearts of millions of fans.

I sat in front of my television, awestruck. I had just seen an example of how exceptional an individual can be. I had seen a group of world class runners placed on a level playing field, and one of them given an extreme disadvantage. But that runner, handicapped though he was, proved that any obstacle can be overcome. It is a lesson that stays with me to this day. Sometimes a person is born who will defy all expectations.

XI-I

I was resigned to the idea of hard labor at the work center. So I was pleasantly surprised to end up working at a clothing warehouse. It is a place nearby which I had seen and heard about from others. A shelter counselor had recruited me to work 36 hours per week for two weeks. Of course I took it. I would be indoors, with a controlled environment, lifting nothing heavier than clothes.

I arrived at seven o'clock in the morning on Monday. The first thing I had to do was fill out a time sheet, then clock in. I talked with the manager, who told me that my reputation preceded me. He was glad to have me on board for two weeks to cover for some people who were on vacation. I was glad too. This was a nice break from the labor intensive work which I had been doing. "What is needed on this job..." he said, "is a steady hand, close attention to the task, and to obey the safety rules."

Most of the people at this huge facility are from the neighborhood. Ironically though, as soon as I walked into my section, I recognized some faces from the shelter. They appeared to fit right in with the work environment. Housing status did not seem to be an issue here. This was good because I did not know what kind of stigma would be attached with my tenure.

I met a foreman on the floor who told me that I would be operating the box binder. Before we began, I had to get set up with the payroll secretary. She took my social security number, had me sign some work forms, and advised me of my salary: one which I was surprised to find was a dollar above minimum wage. Their file showed my home address as the shelter, and that I held a B.A. degree. It occurred to me that Mrs. Lehman, the counselor had been generous with her praise. So, I had her to thank for this comparatively pleasant situation.

Nearly two hours passed and I had not lifted a finger. The next two hours I spent watching the foreman operate the binding machine. As it happens, it's not much of an operation. The actual mechanics of the machine kick in about once every hour. That is when a steel binding strap is placed around a large bundle of cardboard boxes and tightly binds them. The majority of the work is breaking the boxes down and placing them inside the binder. Needless to say I became an expert after the first hour.

A big safety concern on this job is the drop chute that hangs about thirty feet above us. Empty boxes are taken up by conveyer belt to the chute then dropped onto a pile behind us. I was given a hard hat to wear so there would be no serious injuries. Working at the pace of the conveyer belt, I simply broke down boxes, and placed them in the binder.

And then, surprise...surprise...lunch break! Everybody on my floor grabbed a sandwich and went outside. They found awnings and shade trees across the street and prepared to relax for the next forty minutes.

That first day on the job, a resident named Raymond walked up and said "Hey man! You doin' alright so far?"

I said "Yeah, I'm doin' great!" "You didn't bring lunch!"

I said "No!"

"Me neither man! C'mon, let's go back to the dining room!"

So I learned that the time it takes to walk from the warehouse to the shelter; eat lunch, and then walk back was exactly forty minutes.

The next three hours flew by. I was not able to improve on the number of bundles per hour, but I made some other improvements. I sorted out boxes that were comparable in size. That way, when they were compressed inside the binder, they came out in a stack that was neater, tighter, and and contained a greater number of collapsed boxes. A lever inside the binder kicked the bundle over onto a palette.

As a result of the more compact bundle, the forklift did not tilt, nor as I had been warned, drop the bundle on my head.

When the bell rang for end of day, I was relieved. Not because the work day was over, but because I did not have to go to the labor center for the rest of the week.

Arriving back at the shelter I was greeted by Ms. Lehman and another counselor. They had just ended their day as well. They smiled and she asked if I were satisfied with the jobsite. I told them that I was! Pleasantly so! Afterall, I'm not covered with sweat and dust; I'm not totally exhausted; and I am not racked with pain. They got a big laugh from my explanation as they nodded in agreement. Then they were on their way home.

The week seemed to go by before I realized it. By Friday morning I went to work looking forward to the weekend. When we got back from lunch break, I was greeted by a new helper: none other than Mr. Long. Our conversation went as follows!

"Well, well, Mr. Long. How are you?"

"Well, hey Brother Al! I'm only what the savior wants me to be, and that's always good enough for me!"

"Well now Mr. Long, this work is not exactly what's blowing through those doors."

"Oh for sure Brother Al, I know this ain't a breeze! The good book say's there's no work as hard as the lord's work!"

"Okay then! Do you know what to do?"

"Brother Al..., he that does not know the lord's work on this earth, will not be known at the Pearly Gates!"

XI-II

For the first time since my homeless odyssey began, I am feeling a little bit at ease. This weekend is one in which I resided peacefully. I steadied my thoughts as usual by doing crossword puzzles. Not surprisingly, I finished my puzzle book and went shopping for another. The other residents did not bother me at this point. They gave their typical greetings, and let that suffice. Our clashing worlds, it seemed, had finally reached an impasse.

They had become used to the idea that one of them was always hard at work. And when not at work, he's concentrating on crossword puzzles.

At the same time, the notion that I was setting the wrong example is running out of steam. The past week is evidence of that. I see now that our shelter has more resources than I gave them credit for. Again, I am caught off guard. Not only do they have inroads to places like the warehouse, but they can also get easy work for long term residents such as Mr. Long.

But I was not stressed over it. In fact I was glad for them. The little money they earned paid for their residence, as well as offset their passion for begging. This collection of humanity was becoming essentially, not my responsibility. Nevertheless, I had them to deal with. My way of doing things could not make a difference in their lives. And their ways, seemingly, will never change.

The patio is still the center of social life, and gibberish is still the language of choice. The person who talked the loudest was the person who got all the attention. Their subject matter never changed. It was always the what, where, and how about women. Apparently, there are more ways to use and to please a woman than I ever imagined.

On those occasions when I showed up on the patio it was never for a longer time than to have a cigarette. If I worked on my crosswords book I could hear little remarks about my presence at the shelter. I could hear Suggestions that I'm too smart to find my own place.

Maybe some of it is true. Maybe I dwelled so much on the world at-large that my own situation has become insignificant. I wondered sometimes if I needed to be more aggressive towards getting away from this place. And more importantly, I should be more aggressive towards getting away from them.

When my old friend Jean was still at the shelter, I had a better handle on being there. I could lounge around the patio with impunity. All I had to do was back up whatever Jean said. And the only thing Jean ever said was to make observations on what everyone else was saying.

For example, someone commented on a bicycle that Carswell, a part-time carpenter had just ridden onto the yard. "Lord... that jammy is ripped!"

Jean responded: "Yeah... your jammy's more ripped than mine used to be!"

And I quipped: "Yeah, those wheels are straight!"

And so it went! Back and fourth, hour by hour, day in, day out!

XI-III

Jean had at some point in life, reconciled himself with this venue. A certified drifter, he seemed to blend right in with the group. Everyone looked forward to his simple input. Yet his strong suit was his anonymity.

He claims to have been to every state in North America. It is a claim which I am reluctant to dispute. It's very possible that he has gone to many of those places. His familiarity with them seems to bear that out.

Over a period of sixty years a person can have travelled all around the world. Although I can make no such claim, there is no reason to disbelieve this gentleman. He works his way around the center and all of its support systems with ease. It is as if everything is arranged for his needs. He is a person who is not opposed to being legitimized by the providers.

I have been, and always will be opposed to their help. What this establishment has to offer is not what I deem a viable alternative. For some it is the only alternative. But it is not for me. I will never have to wonder why. It's clear that I was born to be hard working and scholarly enough to pursue independent goals.

The brief periods of relaxation which I encounter at the shelter are not to be confused with correlation. It is better, as I say than sleeping in the park Through it all..., I remain... unaccustomed!

XI-IV

The reality of being a drifter has many faces. I have heard stories that range from being on the run with the law, to being on a holy pilgrimage, to getting away from it all.

In the historical definition we know that humans at one time were all nomadic wanderers. It is widely held that our earliest ancestors were nomads. This infers that wandering is in our nature. When people are on the move we stand upright. All of our important senses are at the most advantageous positions. Our eyes affix straight forward to show a three dimensional effect. Our ears, nose, and mouth are up top and facing forward as well giving us easily recognizable facial features. Our brains assess the logic in what our sensory organs receive, thus telling us the smartest thing to do.

When people set out to wander there is no guarantee. Nothing is for certain. We never know for sure what is out there. We know that a space lies between where we are and where we are going. We will know for sure what is out there when we get there. Man is physiologically well suited to rove and roam. We have an inherited curiosity about trails. That's not to say that we know where the trail will lead. It is more to feel assured that the path has been trod before. It is more natural to follow an old trail than it is to blaze a new one.

The size of the human brain has changed over eons. Man's justifications for roaming have changed as well. The only thing that has not changed is his ability to do so. To be a wanderer is to be connected to the ancient past. To roam and rove is to take part in our mission on earth. No matter how civilized we become, we never judge too harshly a person who is a drifter.

Hitchhikers, drifters, wanderers and the sort, go unnoticed. They slip in through the cracks, and slide out under radar without consequence.

Average citizens are reluctant to speak to strangers: especially strangers of no means. Most drifters are absolutely harmless as they march through life. However, most locals cannot be certain of that fact. So drifters are left alone to their devices.

There is no formal school or expertise for their methods of survival. I obtained some information on the subject from conversations which I happened to overhear. I have heard references made to tent colonies. Fellows who did not pass the scrutiny of our shelter counselors were directed by other residents to alternative sites. Those were campsites or colonies whose exact locations I cannot divulge.

XI-V

I have inside information on several sites. The most populous one exists somewhere along the big river. Living there requires specific equipment. The area is on a low lying river bed. The ground is normally damp. Most people who stay here use waterproof sleeping bags. It is heavily forested on all sides. Access is difficult without a scouting axe.

Other large camps lay under highway flyovers. It is said that you should come or go after dark. No one would be happy if their camp was uncovered by the law and razed apart.

I am surprised to learn about the existence of such places. With all my education, I confess that this aspect had escaped me. To figure out that such places existed, I would have needed to know why. Why are places like these encampments necessary? The answer of course is, to meet the needs of drifters.

This of course is far from the reality of most citizens. However, as the cultural efforts of mankind transpire, it is an alternative means of surviving. Though not the preferred means, no one at the sites has been forced to go there. They are there by choice. Clearly, there are some psycho-social forces which have affected those choices. But this alternative route has been taken upon the campers' own volition.

A person living at encampments is not subject to judgments of society at- large. The manner in which they go about their business is done outside the scrutiny of most of us. It would not benefit any of us to leave our comfortable homes in order to see to the well being of persons at encampments. Our practice has been to avoid them, and wish them a bon-voyage.

XI-VI

A wanderer like jean for example, might find himself in a large city. Perhaps he ends up in a place such as Cleveland, or Minneapolis, or Pittsburg. He might get established there for a brief time; finding support systems over the weeks and months. He might attempt to find some social niche. There are lots of bars and the like where a wanderer might blend in, appear commonplace, and confront some old demons.

After a few weeks the loud voices once happy and gay, become mute. They come to represent a different sense. The laughter is undermined by some old feelings of inadequacy. He begins to feel as though other people don't want him there. Maybe he was never meant to be there at all. Inevitably the only solution is to leave. His one choice is to hit the road. Leave quietly one morning to look for a better way. He needs to find some place more accommodating than where he just left. Maybe then, the memories of bad times will not come back with such a rush. Now is his chance to escape; to get back on the freeway!

He slips back into the trade he knows best. Hitchhiking! A long and winding path lies ahead. He walks very far. Then he hitchhikes even farther. What does one search for? Maybe he would like a warmer climate. A smaller city may be a welcome change of pace. Perhaps someplace in Florida, Texas, or Arizona will be better. On the way there, he might touch down in several different locales. He may find happiness in some places, sadness in others. He feeds himself any way that he can. He does odd jobs. He forages, steals bits of food, and begs.

As it has done in the past, getting on the road clears his head. By escaping overwhelming images in his mind, he is able to envision other places. He starts to forget about his past failures.

For some inexplicable reason he no longer feels trapped. There is something about the road which causes him to believe there is new hope.

Along the way, maybe sometime in the near future, he can realize a situation where it is possible to stay in one place. At this stage unfortunately, his only consolation is to remain adrift.

Like so many others, he winds his way across the country unimpeded. He has learned through being there that he will survive.

XI-VII

There exists a virtual drifter highway that only a true practitioner can matriculate. There is even a 'drifter support system' in place. He scans his new locale for another person of his lifestyle. They find each other and begin to exchange information. Word of mouth is the key to their fortunes. The information being passed along will never be seen on billboards, or any other media. Patrons of this system depend solely upon each other. The information has to be accurate. Truth and honor are their only real possessions.

He is told about a nearby church serving hot meals at noon; a Salvation Army Center where he can get a shower and a bed for the night; and a restaurant that gives away dated bread.

This system is not to be confused with the local tourist information boards. It is the reliance that one person has upon another for their unorthodox lifestyles.

Our wanderer gets directed to a local inner-city meals facility. He is comforted to find that he can get dinner every day without issue. He blends in with a large contingent of diners. He hears the loud ranting of local freeloaders as well as some who are just passing through. The information he comes away with will determine his next move. For his purposes it is all- important. Information of the sort is pertinent to his way of life.

XII-I

No matter where egos reside, a person does not want to feel trod upon. Most people strive to work themselves from under foot. Someone who feels that he is being stepped on, simply hopes that there will be a way out. Whether he is a person who believes the world is out to get him, or whether he believes he is the most fabulous person who ever lived, he might still feel that situations are not right for him.

By coincidence, he may seek answers from the persons around him. By virtue of his own hopes and fears he may seek answers from within. All things considered, he should not become too comfortable until he is satisfied that he has done his best. He is trying to resolve any discomfort in his life. He therefore must feel assured that there exists the capacity for betterment. Failing these efforts would be a disaster. If the worst has not yet happened, then heaven help us when it does. Failing to find answers at home, one sets as his goal, finding them someplace else. If no one provides the answers he seeks, his life becomes a quest.

Just as prevalent as our physical environment, other challenges lie inside us. We are never totally happy with situations. The fact that things are always changing means that there is sometimes good, and there is sometimes bad. We must always try to affect our environment because we are the ones who must live in it. We confront the challenges of day to day living, and we put upon them our own remedies. We are best advised to approach every day with care. Since we do not know the future, we must hope that we can bring about better things.

Civilized beings use knowledge in order to best approach their environment. We look at both the distant past and recent events to figure out where we are going. We rely on our sciences, trades, and religions for inspiration. We want to be all knowing. But our universe is infinite to the extent that we will never embrace everything about it. We need to take life slowly and to be as studious as possible.

It is not our mission to face the past but to face the future. There is much about the past which stirs our curiosity. Still we must fixate on that view of the universe which gives us the best insight on what is to come.

Slowly but surely we make sense of our places. We have to believe that we are in the right place at the right time. If we do not, we will find ourselves prey to those conditions that make life regrettable.

Can everyman be optimistic? No! Yet we have to remain optimistic about every man's chances. We must believe that we are in pursuit of happiness. We therefore seek to envision those things which put us and the world around us, in the best way.

XII-II

We have the ability not only to have thoughts, but also to record those thoughts in writing. Let's not take that ability lightly. Let us as well show proper respect for those who take writing to task.

AL'S APOLOGY ON WRITING

PURE CREATIVITY IS BEING
IN HARMONY WITH SOMETHING UNKNOWN.
THEN EVERY LIVING THING BECOMES
A PERFECTLY AGITATED SPORE.
ITS LIVING ENVIRONMENT SPINS AND
BENDS AND FLOATS; CHARGED WITH UNIVERSAL
IONS, AND POTENTIAL TO BE MORE.

NEAR PERFECTION REPRODUCES ITS
IMPERFECT CELLS IN SUIT OF FIXING
THAT WHICH NATURE AND TIME HAVE DEEMED GONE.
DEFINED BY FORM AND ARMORED FOR SCOPE,
IDEAS BRACE, EXTEND, AND PROLONG.
HERE EVENTUALLY BECOMES NOWHERE;
LEST ONE FINDS ANOTHER PLACE TO ABSCOND.

UNLESS ONE FINDS WHAT HE IS SEEKING
AT SUCH A PLACE, HE MAY NEVER REST.
IT'S AS IF EVERY LIVING THING
FLEW OUT OF A UNIVERSAL WHOLE,
AND SEPARATELY THEY HAVE NO QUEST...
AS IF THEY MUST ALWAYS KEEP MOVING;
TO BE THE BRIGHTEST, AND SEEK THE BEST.

LANGUAGE: ESSENCE OF IMPERCTION
AND EXCLUSIVE PROPERTY OF MAN;
LEADS US FARTHER AND FARHER ASTRAY.
IT DECEIVES BROTHERS, FOOLS THE MASSES,
AND CONFUSES MEN FROM FAR AWAY.
WRITING LANGUAGE IS THE ART OF
THOSE WHO PERFECT US FOR ONE MORE DAY.

XII-III

When we put our spoken language into writing we give ourselves the facility to recall our deeds. Actions that had disappeared from word of mouth transitions are forever maintained in written form. Writing is a more visible form of language. Speaking is man's burden. Writing gives us the wherewithal to manage it. Speaking actually can be any kind of babble. We only need to give it meaning or sense. Any sound that rolls off the human tongue is speaking. The words of men are always taken as having some kind of meaning. It is easy for a speaker to blurt out a string of words. It takes a higher degree of intent to put that same notion into writing.

Written language may also be intended to serve those not within earshot. As a consequence, it tends to be more formal in presentation. It often is more sincere in believability. Therefore writing becomes more contractual. We can depend on what we read. Receipts, labels treaties, essays, certifications, listings, and so on are perceived as having validity. When writing in any language reaches its ultimate sophistication, it can be romanticized and formulated for stories and plays.

I have an affinity for reading. I tend to believe what I read. As long as memory serves me I have been in love with the English alphabet system. I learned at an early age how to match letter sounds to the words that I read. I could always read anything that an adult could read. My only limitation was with vocabulary. I would ask my mother about the meanings of words that I pronounced. One day she bought a new set of encyclopedia. I immediately lost myself in reading. I have often imagined that she bought those books as a ruse to get me out of her hair.

My propensity in linguistics is a natural state. It was developed and reinforced by my parents. I was coddled, encouraged, and then ultimately left to my own devices. Today I read, write, and do crossword puzzles as a way of revivifying one of my fondest passions.

If I were a true drifter, I would have written about it. There would be no questions as to environment, behavior, mentality, or social surroundings. Everything of significance will have been dutifully noted. There would be a perfect record of deeds compiled by a drifter with first hand experience from having done that. Readers could see for themselves the highlights and tribulations of daily life.

In reality though, all information that I relate is being done in a second-hand light. It is hearsay! My written reports are those of someone with no first-hand experience. My insights are fed by the personal relationships I have with those who have actually roved and roamed. Relationships I say as opposed to friendships. The problem with maintaining these kinds of relationships is the tenuousness of it all. More often than not, the information I hear is involuntary. In an effort to avoid being a full fledged participant, I ignore the brethren with whom I come into contact. But out of the situations that I cannot ignore, comes perpetual information.

Subsequently, I keep to those ways that identify me as a hearty participant in polite society. Steps which I have taken to maintain these ways appear to be correct so far. The things I have done are the best possible, under the circumstances.

Outside forces have had their impact. I contended with them as well as can be expected. To speculate about their effects on where I am is all that I can do. I would say that to an extent, I am comparatively well-off.

We must assume that others around us are in competition for resources. As we go on in life, we expect to maintain a comfortable living for ourselves and our families. We hope to avoid having to do backbreaking work all our lives.

All of these things apply to the definition of being of sound mind. Every man assumes that his neighbors are in pursuit of similar goals. I have always assumed that. I have always believed that the normal thing to do is compete with others for better jobs, higher wages, and more material possessions. The person who does not fall somewhere in this broad scheme is abnormal.

Every man is purported to have been given an equal chance to succeed. In our contemporary world, this is almost true. Paradoxically, not every man has been shown the same path to success.

We know that that there are barriers. They vary in scope and in degree. They differ from social, to mental and physical. They remain steadfast from ethnic status to individual ability. A person may live his entire life in the upper class community where he was born without ever visiting the black hole of deprivation that exists across county lines.

Not everyone is possessed of what we define as equal opportunity. For some of us, the first challenge is to perceive ourselves as capable beings. As our diligent speaker Mr. Long once said, "God's joy is to be shared by every man."

A small segment of our society has chosen to not participate. They have opted out of the rat race. They see that typical concepts are not the way to go. Those persons have selected a more simplistic way to survive.

If he is upset with the establishment, or whether he has issues of his own is a matter for that individual. Subsequently, he and others like him will be categorized and labeled. In due course they are thrown together as a non- glorified lot. They become a social order that we can easily identity with a word like "bum".

Our cultural beliefs allow us to feel that such a definition can suffice. It allows us to instinctively respond when a friend points out a bum. Without much thought we say, "let's go somewhere else."

We have rationalized that: 'I am not my brother's keeper'; or that, 'God helps those who help themselves.' Yet these notions continue to push contemporary man another step farther away from his tribal ancestors. Dealing with modern complexities makes it impossible to give support to a vagabond person. Unlike past cultures, our own success is so important that we view someone who fails with abhorrence.

What has compelled their simpler lives? Admittedly, most of us don't know. We cannot understand why someone gives up; what facets are guiding him; what's hindering his ways. Does this individual lack intelligence enough to survive in today's world? Does that person have an alternative motive for portraying himself as bum?

All the above questions could be dealt with on case by case bases. But at the end of the day, such individuals are giving themselves to categorization. The effect of bonding and allegiance is to strengthen their low status.

We must not confuse their sub-society with persons who are experiencing a temporary setback. I have met a college professor at this shelter. He is said to be waiting for severance paychecks before he can move on to another school. He was terminated one semester ago due to a lack of interest in his ancient pottery class.

I have met another gentleman who is suffering from the long term effects of his service in the Viet Nam war. Kelly was slightly wounded in battle and he never fully recovered. Some ten years afterward he suffered a debilitating stroke. He has no feeling on the side of his body where a bullet grazed his head.

He struggles to walk, but can get to where he wants to go. His speech has been severely hampered but he can be understood by anyone who takes the time to hear what he is saying. His overall prognosis is positive. He is personable and outgoing.

At the shelter, all of Kelly's needs are met. And to our government's credit, all of his financial needs are met as well. He does not view his brethren at the shelter as bums. In fact each person is a potential friend. He is easily recognizable and well liked.

In lieu of his special needs, his presence at this place is understandable. He still does not function well enough to live on his own.

To some he is an American hero. To others who don't know all the facts, he is a gimp. To still others who see him hanging out with his friends, he is a bum. Kelly has learned over a brief period to mimic the behaviors of those around him. But unlike most of those men, Kelly sometimes is visited by his family. And periodically he goes home. Kelly has found his niche at the shelter. He enjoys being there.

But for Kelly there is a light at the end of the tunnel. Every time he walks across the yard, to the store, or to the park, he is getting physical therapy. Each time he struggles to verbalize his thoughts, he is exercising speech centers. Even if a full recovery is not in the cards for him, Kelly works hard everyday at just that.

Such persons as Kelly and the professor can be viewed as participating in a system which supports bums. But they must not be viewed as participants in that sub-society who has opted to live a simpler style of life.

XIII-1

I have developed a personal theory of what causes homelessness, though I am reluctant to publicize. The more I reflect upon it, the more sarcastic it feels. I surmise that my theory is nothing more than circumstances under which I have contrasted the lives of those individuals with that of my own. I have looked at my hard working ways as the key to lifting myself out of the sand. Conversely, I viewed the lazy fare pervading the shelter as the workshop of the devil.

I believe that those persons are perpetuating their own failures in life. Upon further consideration, I know that I cannot cast a blanket over all those individual situations. Any theory I put forth could only ascribe negativity. Every man has his own cross to bear. When and how he does it is according to his own capacities to cope. I can cite a personal history of working that goes back to the young age of thirteen. I used to help my grandmother during summer breaks at her shop in New York.

To get there from my home in Georgia, I learned to travel by Greyhound bus. It was not difficult in those days to imagine that I was a drifter. In reality though, I could have made the trip with any one of my adult family members. So I cannot actually say that I have been a drifter. I will only say that I was in league with the spirit of being a drifter.

XIII-11

I chose to ride the bus in order to be free of family members. When I travelled alone I could thoroughly absorb the environment. I was free to make assessments based on what I saw, not on what others were telling me. I could then draw my own conclusions.

The enlightenment I perceived came resonating from speaker systems on the bus. I pondered why it was necessary for the driver to open microphones and tell us where we were going. After all, every person on the bus had purchased a ticket to a destination. It could have been that not everyone was as comfortable as I with barreling down the highway.

Or maybe some passengers needed to be reassured that the bus driver knew exactly where he was going. They had to put aside any doubts about the ride and their safety in getting there. I, on the other hand knew exactly where we were because I had seen those roads before.

Then the bus would leave those long, familiar highways and take to some smaller, less familiar routes. From there I could see the people a little better. I could see that two or three of them had reached their destinations. The bus had pulled into a small town and a passenger announced..."O.K. everybody, this is us. Y'all have a blessed trip!" And many others responded. "Thank you honey: Bye, bye!"

The leaving passengers seemed relieved to be back home. They appeared to me to be the right kind of persons for their town. It was a happy event for all involved. The passengers waiting to board told me a different story. They had a more adamant demeanor about themselves. I could see the determination etched on their faces. This trip would be in all seriousness. I perceived a look that said "I am on the road to bigger and better things." This time there would be no turning back.

Anytime I am on the road, the star of the show is always the landscape. Local roads are invariably lined with orchards, fields, and crops of some type. Periodically, between the rows of cotton, peaches, watermelon, and beans, a street would appear. These will have held another distraction in life. They are testimony to the ability of man to do the Lord's work on this earth.

Streets would appear that lead to who knows where. They seemed to go on for hundreds of miles. Until finally the driver said..."OoooKaay, all passengers: Now arriving...in Fayetteville! This will be a thirty minute stopover! You may leave the bus for a short break. Please have your tickets in hand when re-boarding. FAYETTEVILLE!"

The town of Fayetteville, N.C. is along Interstate-95. I have been there many times enroute to New York. It was a welcome stop along our way. It is different though from the perspective of being a bus passenger. I got the chance to walk around for awhile, and see some sights. My main priority was to avoid being lost. I strolled a few blocks, making sure to stay on the same street. I encountered some nightclubs and bars long the way. I looked at my wristwatch and made a U-turn.

When I arrived at the bus I was greeted by the driver. Looking at my ticket, he said "Got a long way to go, don't you?" "Yes!" I said. "You're a good driver!" He laughed! "Ha, ha, ha...thanks buddy! Well, let's get this show back on the road!" Although the bus moves at about the same rate of speed as my father drives, we were getting from point (A) to point (B) at a critically slower pace. By the time we arrived in Raleigh/Durham, I had seen everything I needed to see.

At the age of thirteen I chose to travel from Georgia to New York by Greyhound Bus.

I fell asleep and did not move again until someone awakened me. It was the bus driver telling me that we had to change to another bus. The sun was up. At least five hours had passed and we were in Richmond. A city on I-95, it was another familiar stop. In those days it was more recognizable for its domes and toll booths than for its present day high rise office buildings.

"Two hours!" the driver said. "... Gate seven!" I grabbed my knapsack and walked out. I strolled down the block. I kept myself oriented to where I was: on Broad Street; two hours to kill. I had breakfast in a small café. Then I found some pinball machines. This is memorable for me because I recall playing pinball with some kids my age.

Time flew by and I was back on the bus. The trip had been very edifying for me up to that point. I had seen this part of the world in its bare essentials: a much larger place than I could have imagined. More importantly, I learned some things about myself. It was all too clear that I could do this journey alone. The same confidence that my parents had in me, I now had in myself.

I briefly wondered what it would be like if I were to take the bus going west, rather than staying on the one going north. What would it be like to go some place I had never before been? Would I find the same rural settings? Would there be mile after mile of plowed fields? If I changed my way, what would lay around the next bend?

Just as I was about to envision what those roads would be like, we came into Alexandria, Virginia. This was my call back to reality. Once you get across the Potomac River, the pace changes quickly. Now in D.C., things are faster and happen more rapidly. It was time for me to be alert.

I pulled my knapsack from the overhead compartment and set it on my lap.

This time I did not leave the bus. I kept my place as it filled to capacity.

The same routine goes in Baltimore one hour later. People scrambled for a seat. They appeared to have a list of choices to make. First on the list: who to sit next to; second, who would take the window seat; finally, they chose whether this would be a loud rowdy trip, or a peaceful ride.

To my relief, the boisterous crowd became quieter as we got farther away from Old Baltimore. Except for the matter of having to elbow some guy, things were going smoothly. I didn't mind his snoring, but I objected to him using my shoulder for a pillow. There would be no tussling match on this trip.

In no time at all, here they were: Henry, Richard, Walter, Zeke...a cadre of cousins. What a sight for sore eyes. Every one of them wore a broad smile. All were eager for the fun and the foolishness to begin. "Helll...llloooo NEW YORK!"

Grandma Rosie had shown up too. I was so happy to see her. Even so, she made herself clear from the start. "Knock it off boys! I won't put up with a lot of foolishness." Of course we obeyed. It had been almost a year since I had been with them.

During that time away, I lost some of my need to play around. I had grown taller than Rosie, and I was more cognizant of other people around me.

The long bus ride was a real eye opener. It helped me decide how I need to present myself to others. I must demonstrate that I am a person of responsibility. I must carry my own weight. I have to behave as though no one is more responsible for me than me.

And so with a single glance, I could visualize the entire summer. I saw a formidable agenda ahead. For example, I had to touch base with Grandma Amy. I am certain she felt I would be spending most of my time with her. She and the other side of my family live in a different part of town. They seemed to view me as the second coming of my father; only bigger, smarter, and with greater potential.

My older brother Syl, with whom I spent last Christmas, will also be around. He and my two nephews will be making every car ride an intellectual foray. Every place we visit seems to have a function in the big picture. He tends to lecture about things we do, and I tend to listen. This summer, I will put my own spin on things.

For the most part though I will be with Rosie. I will be working in her store. This year I want to earn more money. I no longer can subsist on the chump-change that my parents sometimes gave to me. My needs go beyond those amounts. I want some new sneakers; Converse All-Stars, to be exact. My basketball game is starting to come around.

I must have the right equipment. And of a more artistic need, I want to purchase a better guitar. My mother gave me a nylon stringer for my ninth birthday. I have mastered it. It now has become more of a toy, but it has unlocked my subdued passion for music. All my siblings and I were taught to play my mother's piano. Stephen, Jr. became very proficient. I chose the guitar for my sessions. I loved what I could do. It has led me to desire a larger more resonant nylon stringed instrument. I saw one that I liked at a music store in Savannah. I picked it up and began to play "Green Sleeves". The customers started to applaud, and some were teary-eyed. Only, I didn't have the two hundred dollar price tag.

XIII-V

I felt like a piece of inventory as I stood next to Rosie. People milled around touching the fruit, creating sandwiches, and staring at me. It was okay though because I stared right back at them. Rosie would turn to me and whisper things..."smile sometimes!"

It seemed everyday that went by, I was given some kind of advice... "Don't fold your arms!" "Get her to buy something more!" One day I said to her: "Rosie, you're the consummate professional." But she wasn't laughing. "Don't think I can't spank your ass!"

Rather than make a scene, I let her have the last word. My paycheck was the most important thing. As to which, she was very generous.

XIV-I

At a single glance backwards, I could recall the entire summer. It was not easy to put my accomplishments into perspective. I lay there at home just listening to the sounds around me. I was very comfortable with the way that I was accommodated. Not inclined to draw any conclusions, I was satisfied with the job I had done. I was happy that I met all my goals.

So where do I go from here? I go back to Georgia, obviously. It is a fact that was decided for me before the entire issue began. The summer now past was only part of the plan for me. This comfort zone is about to become unhinged.

The process of being in this place at this time has taken me down the road of valuable experiences. Not only were my objectives met; I was at best eased.

Yet I could see the hands of my parents at work. I could see their concern for my overall development. I could hear them on the telephone with my New York family. I could imagine what they were saying about me.

[Rosie]-"What is he doing?" "Where is he going?"

[Mom]-"He wants a job" "He's not old enough to work."

[Rosie]-"Just send him to me." "Don't worry!"

[Mom]-"Okay momma, we'll do it like that."

I don't know if I would have had the wherewithal to plot and carry out such a move on my own. Probably not! So I should be grateful for the success of this endeavor. I should therefore not just say goodbye to Rosie, but also show my gratitude. I will say thank you for the opportunity to learn what they had to teach.

I must infer from this summer that I benefitted greatly. Our strong family ties are what got me to where I am. I cannot demonstrate any motives that show otherwise.

XIV-II

As this grand universe would have it, there exists opportunities to stray. When I consider all that goes on around me every day, straying from the path is a part of the cycle. There are so many ways to get off the planned path. For one, I might drop out of school. I doubt however, this is an option for me. Everyone I know would go into total shock.

Yet I know some school aged people who do not attend school at all. These are kids who do nothing all day but hang out. I hear that they steal what they need or sell drugs to make a living. Some children are induced by others to quit school. Under the proper circumstances, children can easily fall prey to outside influences. They crave the comradeship and simple lifestyle. That is why the motivational objectives of our public schools systems must always remain in step.

Children place their well being in the hands of adults. It is difficult for them to deduce when they are being misled by those whom they trust. They are subject to believe and do as they are told. It takes only the issue of trust to convince them they are doing the right thing.

Sometimes a child may have fooled his parents. He may have led them to believe that he is in school when he is actually not. It is an easy deception if the parents leave home for work before school begins; then return home after it ends. The child hides out at home, and the parents are none the wiser. If so, the child's truancy is their faults. They are not making sincere efforts to insure that the child is doing what is required of him. In which case, any kind of misfortune can occur.

I witnessed an incident once at parent teacher night when a father began punching and kicking his son. I heard later that none of the boys scheduled teachers had ever seen him before.

Someone who departs school prematurely, misses the formal events which graduates experience. The earlier the departure, the more difficult it is for a person to identify with their age group. Someone who drops out of eighth ngrade will experience puberty alone. When a boy's voice starts to change, and he sees evidence of a beard, there will be no classmates to share the event with. When a young lady experiences her first monthly cycles, she won't have a classroom full of other girls to consult with.

A child quits school early because he or she wants to get away from the rigors of eighth grade courses. Most children, if they could would avoid math, history, writing, vocabulary, and the like. They are confronted by those skills on a daily basis nonetheless.

Our young drop out boy is recruited to work at lawn care. He is promised twenty five percent of one hundred dollars. When the job is finished, he is given twenty dollars. He walks away satisfied, unaware that his friends have taken advantage of his inability to do math.

Our young lady jots down directions to a potential client's house. On the bus, she tells the driver that she is a babysitter who needs to find an address. She shows him what she had written down. The driver says to her "I can't understand your writing!" She realizes that her spelling is less than adequate, her usage is inappropriate, and her sentence structure makes no sense at all.

These young people are not aware of the harm they have done themselves. They have no reason ironically to say "I've made a mistake." At such a young age, their decision to quit school is not yet a bad idea. They may still see a light at the end of the tunnel. All their best years are in front of them. Youth is their greatest ally. Anything that can go wrong, has the potential in time to be set right.

The youngster is confident in his ability to buck the system. He proved them wrong before when he successfully quit school. He will prove them wrong again when he takes control of his own fate, and becomes the best that he can be.

Unfortunately he is not yet mature enough to fully appreciate his predicament. The studious path which had been so carefully planned for him is now twisted and unclear. He compromised his right to learn and grow in a formal system. Having left the path, he increased his own risks by a huge number.

All is not lost however. Success has many faces. It could mean becoming a high level drug dealer, or a top flight extortionist: skills they don't teach you in school. It will also mean a "paper trail." I would prefer to be represented by the paper trail which presently identifies me. For example, my middle league baseball team had its photo in the newspapers. We won three consecutive championships. Our names and positions were listed. I also have access to all school transcripts; elementary through college.

The paper trail for someone other than myself could appear much less desirable. Specifically, a person who chose to quit school may end up listed in Juvenile Detention incidents. From there they would likely go to A-F-I-S (Automated Fingerprint Identification Systems). There might also be an arrest record which further complicates ones life.

When I look back at the way things unfolded this summer, its hard to imagine that everything happened by chance. My mother and grandmother had it all arranged. I am not envious because they control my life. They created me; I am their responsibility. I am a product of their upbringing; of their environment.

What I ultimately will become, resides with me. Although my being is well defined, I have the ability to resist. It would be hard to disappoint my loved ones. But I could if I so desired.

I must determine at this age whether or not the guidance I am receiving is that which will suit me best. To that end, I can say that I am happy with who I am.

There are many factors pertaining to development. They can be either mental, physical, emotional, genetic, social, and so forth, or all of the above. I am similar to my mother and father because they are the ones who passed on my traits. It is a combination of the two which causes me to be neither one nor the other. The way in which I interpret my world; the way in which that world impacts my life, are considerations which apply, to my own personal abilities.

The adoration I have for my guitar is unique to me. At the same time, all my siblings are musically inclined. Our passion for the arts is a family trait. My being different from others in my family only means that I prefer the guitar. When I see my brother Stephen expressing himself on the keyboards, or my brother Earl creating sculpture from clay, they seem to be different from me and from each other. Yet our artistry has come to us from a thousand generations. And we; the present day representatives of that gene pool, are unlikely to shed those qualities. As different as we may appear, we are in a greater sense, not different at all.

Sports are planned activities that keep hyperactive young men and women out of trouble. We all have participated on sports teams. Balls and other sporting equipment are only toys. However they are the best distractions ever created by man. The bonds that exist between members of a sports team, and that which exists between members of an army platoon are the same.

They depend on each other to match up with opposing unit members, run interference, back up teammates, and work their hardest to win. As those games fade into the distant past, just the memory of their unity and their efforts is all that is needed to reaffirm that bond. Many years later, squad members can still count on each other.

Sports for my family is planned to affect a more utilitarian purpose. My eldest brother, my youngest brother, and all of us in between have gotten through college on sports scholarships. The older ones having made their marks took it upon themselves to assist the younger hopefuls. I can truthfully say that we have made our parents proud.

No one of us has strayed from the path. We consider ourselves a hard working strong group. But we are by no means unique in society. All across our nation can be found examples of determined and competitive groups. Whatever it is that's motivating those persons to be strong, I consider a positive trait. I believe that intelligent persons are always aware of the consequences of failure. As such, they work tirelessly to avoid the pitfalls in life.

Most people do not aim to become an emperor. We commonly want to acquire nice things and stay out of financial debt. Toward that end we keep feverishly at work. There are yet others without motivation. There are some who simply have not worked hard enough or have not planned well enough to see at least a modicum of success.

They are pressed to survive on very minimal incomes. Without financial stability they settle for the least desirable accommodations. Worst yet, they are surrounded on all sides by reminders of their shortcomings: meaning other low income persons, depressed dwellings, and lack of attention from local governments. Residents who have been unable to improve their situations might find themselves victims of a wider social phenomenon; part of an evolving constituency living on the fringes of our capitalist societies. They may become part of the group of "disenfranchised:" that which perpetuates the cycle of poverty.

Most of us are disgusted by the existence of poverty. We have an acquired passion for the good life. Most of us would say that we'd prefer having a lot of money as opposed to having a little money. We see it around us so much that most of us can relate to being rich. Paradoxically, someone living in poverty in America is always a short leap from being wealthy. And certainly if a poor person should suddenly become rich, he would know exactly what to do with the money.

He would not have to apply for membership to a higher social class. His only requirement would be to spend the money wisely. First he would need to move out of his oppressed surroundings. Then he would have to drop those persons who in so many ways, had obscured his view of a better life; those who for so long, manifested all the woes of the oppressed.

Once away from his other influences, our "nouveau riche" citizen may prosper. But there is a parable which says "you can take the boy out of the slum, but you can't take the slum out of the boy." It is true to a certain point. And it is why our citizen is most likely to re-visit his poor roots.

He has come a long way; yet he has not gone very far. Despite the good luck, his roots are his sanctuary. All he wants to do is to let his former neighbors know that he is still himself. He might buy a round of drinks; sponsor a taxi ride for a senior friend; or help a buddy with groceries.

He is still plagued however by some eerie feelings. Because he lived in an oppressed environment, he wants to figure out who among the oppressors could have benefitted from his problems. He realizes that he was not only someone's sorrowful friend, but also somebody's goat. And he also has the urge to figure out who among his peers took advantage of his low self esteem; who gave him that debasing nickname; and why he could not see through those long subjugating nights.

XV-II

Our country will never operate as a stratified class system. It was guaranteed in the charters of our founding fathers. We will never have a class of Lords and Ladies, or Dukes and Duchesses to bow to. There will never be an upper crust which hordes and obtains our natural resources. The constitution says that all men are created equal. Our Government is set up to insure the integrity of those laws.

There are no divisions in society that are obvious. There are no juntas, cadres, or unions that are not responsive to someone. Our congressmen for example are free to make laws and dictate funding, but they can be dropped by the voters. Our Supreme Court justices have the final word in judicial matters, but they are appointed not born to their jobs.

Our system, on the surface appears to be the paradigm of all governments.

We appear as the culmination of historically erred governments which contributed bits and pieces to our perfect one. But what lies beneath? Were it not for the malicious politics of ethnicity and race that have divided us from inception, ours would be the model for the final perfect society.

I will not make a statement for radical change however. I am always being told in fact that I am lucky to have been born an American.

I have never longed for the amenities in life. I was privileged to have lots of material things. My siblings and I had everything we needed to keep us distracted. We watched sports on television for most of the day. Then we went outside and organized a game.

When the games were over I would go inside and play with my guitar. I used sheet music to help me with tuning and studying chords. I also collected music books which contained all the popular songs of the day. I amassed a virtual library. From those I could read or play by ear almost any song. People who were lucky enough to hear me play would talk about how brilliant I was.

My favorite artists were George Segovia and Jose Feliciano. I had all of Feliciano's English recordings. His skills on the guitar were unmatched. He was my benchmark. I kept practicing and over the years became satisfied with my abilities.

I am most proud of the acclaim given to me by my youthful colleagues. It was the summer before I went to college. Some buddies who also considered themselves musicians invited me in on a jam session. They didn't know exactly what my skill level was and I had never played with a group. We knocked off a few songs. I did a few solos. And the session was over. I was looking at them, and they were staring at me.

Wilson said "What are you gonna do with that man?" I said "What do you mean?" Tom said "You sound like Feliciano!"

I was suddenly at a loss. That was unusual for me, and I didn't know what to tell them. They were serious about furthering their musical careers. They had plans to move to Atlanta. As for myself, the music was just one of many hobbies. I had mastered my instrument, and I had shone brightly. But that's all it was; just another hobby.

XV-III

My world in those days was an expanding one. Their vote of confidence was all I needed to move on to bigger and better things. The term local in my point of view, meant everything on Interstate-95 between New York and Georgia. I couldn't stay.

No one that I knew had the same experiences growing up as I had. I could talk first hand about travelling on a regular basis. I have been in temperatures ranging from twenty degrees below zero, to temperatures of one hundred and twenty degrees above. I am familiar with highway numbers in Georgia, South Carolina, North Carolina, Virginia, D.C., Maryland, Delaware, Pennsylvania, New Jersey, and New York. I have been to places like The Maryland House, South of the Border, The Baltimore Tunnel, and The New Jersey Turnpike. I never had to wonder if any of my friends had more experiences. Their best information came from me. I could mesmerize them if I so chose, but I preferred not to. I could rub their noses in it, but it's not my style.

On those occasions when I was away for an extended period, I simply let everyone know that I was with family. I have never actually been in a rut in my young life, neither socially, mentally, nor otherwise. I have never had the time to do so.

My youthful dreams were not fantasies. My thoughts were always crisp and on task. They had to be. I had to excel at school, sports, music, reading and behavior. And when those were done, I had to concentrate on the best way to manipulate my environment: one that's so multifaceted, it seemed to contract and expand along with my thoughts. I had to be up to snuff on what was popular to wear and say down south. Those things were always different from what was popular up north. To that end, I was always on top of my game.

Some of the guys were asserting that the air up north is unclean. I believe they were referring to the manufacturing facilities that used to line the New Jersey Turnpike. I admitted that what they had seen on the television was true. The pollution was stifling. It would burn my eyes and sting my nose.

Other friends had heard that there were dead fish floating in the Savannah River. That was also true. The stench would overwhelm anyone who crossed a bridge. From the nuclear plant at Augusta-Aiken, to the manufacturing centers in Savannah, the deadly sludge winded its way to the ocean.

"What about those pizzerias?" someone asked "...are they really that good?" "Uhm-hhm!" I said. "Have you ever had a chopped steak sandwich?" "Oh yes!" I assured them. "But my favorite is a pastrami sandwich. That was my introduction to Kosher Food. It is so delicious. Though I enjoy everything I taste. Sometimes when we eat out, I order curry chicken and dumplings. Sometimes I ask for lasagna and cheesecake."

Someone different would say to me..."Ya'll eat grits all the time down there don't you?" "Oh yes!" I would tell them "it ain't breakfast without grits! And we don't put sugar on them!" I went on..."I like butter and gravy, smoked sausage, fried pork chops, and ground beef cooked in onions." And furthermore I said..."No frozen pancakes!"

"Cops down there like to jack people around..." a friend said. "They call you boy and make you pay them money!" "You're right on that!" I answered. "I can remember a couple of times when I was little, my father got pulled over on a local road. This was before the Interstate was completed in South Carolina and Georgia. My father would pay a fine on the spot. He used to say that he didn't have time to go to court."

"Man, I always hear about police corruption up there." "There's no denying!" I told them. "The Knapp Commission Hearings was the only thing on T.V.! The only good cop is a dead cop I heard."

"Yeah! So what do they do with all that dope they take from people?" "They sniff it!" I said.

We talked a lot about women! Guys have heard things about the girls up north. For example, the girl in that song 'Eyes of a New York Woman'. They ask me about the situation as though I have figured out how those eyes affect men! My response was "I don't know! There's nothing about those eyes that put them on a higher level than other women." Then they would remind me about my eighth grade girlfriend. "Oh, that's right" I said jokingly. "Shelly is from New York. She really had a long cold stare. She used to make me feel like I owed her something." Everyone would laugh. I forgot to mention how hard it was to look away.

Another friend said "Man, there are some healthy looking girls down south!

I'd take one of them over a New York girl any day!"

"Are you asking me or telling me?" I said…"Because I can't see any difference. A good looking woman is a good looking woman! And I ain't trying to give nobody a physical! But then again you make a good point. Clean living can do a lot for a person. And especially for a woman's smile. They're more honest, and more sincere. But I can't say as yet, more beautiful. One of my buddies has a cousin who lives in the New York City area. He tells me his cousin seems to always be alert to things. I agreed with his observation. "You have to be sharp in that part of the world." I explained…"You can't allow yourself to be taken in by what you see and hear. Too often, situations will develop according to your confidence in them. If you go there…" I told them. "…it's best to stay on the beaten path, and keep moving."

"I wish I lived down south!" a friend remarked. "You have a better chance of making something of yourself." To a small extent, he was right. There may be fewer outlets of professional positions, but there are lifestyle nuances which lend themselves to more professionalism. "Young people have a more respectful relationship with adults." I said… "They commit themselves more to the educational system. And frankly, they place more value on the well- being of others."

"But you know Al…" a friend said to me "…there are just too many limitations on what you can get done here in the south. I'm only trying to keep things real. That trip we took last summer, it was really nice. It was short, but it taught me some things I could never learn from postcards."

"Just driving around Philadelphia felt like a weight had been lifted off my shoulders. It was like the cops were somewhere else studying their notes instead of me. It didn't matter where I was going! I was free to move about and take in the view."

"It was like you're actually a part of the law, and not just following it. It's like, when you stop at a traffic light it's because you want the other cars to have their turn to advance. You don't have to feel like you'd better or the cops will pounce on you. When the light changes back, the other cars will allow you to go on your way. The traffic light only exists to help you with your timing."

"I get it!" I said. "You feel like the system is for you!"

"Yeah that's right! I realized I could judge things better when I'm functioning out of common courtesy instead of fear. Also, people there are not bogged down in tradition. Their idea of tradition is to move forward. Ya know Al, if I get the chance again, I think I'm going to stay up north!"

"Yeah..." I said..."why should you not?"

"Ya know what Al?" my cousin in New York said..."it's time for me to turn the page."

"What do you mean?" I said.

"You remember Carl...lived by the stadium!" He's dead!" "What?" I interjected. "What the hell happened?"

"He and his boys robbed a restaurant in Duchess County. The cops chased them down and bumped them off the parkway."

"All I'm saying cous' is that he didn't have to go out like that. He made good money at work. They just have a need to be stupid! The kids in the car with him didn't have a scratch on them. They'll be out of jail next month."

"What I'm saying is that it feels like I'm living in a big jar with a lot of brainless people! I want to live in a smaller jar. That way, I can tell if somebody tries to throw a brick and bust up what I have. And when that jar spins, I can see a different side of the world."

"I think I understand." I nodded. "You want to see what else is out there!" "Al, I just can't take no more! The lying, the distrust, I know I can do better than this. I want to get away from these so-called friends: see things from another angle. I've never set foot out of this town. I think it's time I did. Maybe down south for awhile...you know; like Uncle Stevie did. Hopefully I won't end up in a ditch!" "Yeah!" I said..."Hopefully!"

Our labor crew made it back safe and sound again to the work center. It's been that way ever since I took over the driving chores of the work van. Whenever we had a jobsite that required us to take the van out of town, a member of the crew had to drive. Of the twenty five or more workers who showed up on any given morning, only three of us had a valid driver's license. The person who drove was paid an additional ten dollars. I was a new face at the place compared to the others. When I heard about the extra money, I doubted that there was a chance I could become a driver.

But things happen, and chances go around. The first driver, one morning quit the work crew. He was picked up by a construction company. Certified to operate the jackhammer, he would not touch a jack while signed on with the labor crew. He points out that if he uses his licensed skills as a member of the labor crew, he would get paid minimum wage. When his number had come up, and he finally was called on, he made eight dollars more per hour.

The second guy was a friendly man who worked hard every day. He and his buddies were trapped in the backbreaking world of day-labor because they constantly smoked marijuana. They behaved as though they never grew out of their teens. Here was a group of thirty something year old men, sitting in the back of a work van smoking dope and playing around.

No one really cared what they did. They were harmless enough until it was his turn to drive. The rest of his buddies moved to the front of the van. Meanwhile, the others of us sat staring at the highway. We never had to yell out a warning to them but were on constant lookout. Each time he took his eyes off the road to tell a joke, or took his hands off the steering wheel and drove with his knees, we would cringe.

One morning as I waited for my ride with a private owner vehicle, the van crew came back into the center. They were followed closely behind by the police. The crew driver had gone a few blocks before he crashed the van into a car at a stoplight. He didn't stick around. He sprang from the driver's seat and never stopped running. I heard later that he was somewhere in Florida.

It was subsequently my turn to drive. For a couple of weeks I was the only driver. There were times when I delivered crews to different sites in the mornings. Then afterwards I went back to the shelter with the van. I would sit around until three o'clock in the afternoon, then go back out to pick everybody up.

The only drawback to this situation was that it put me for the better part of the day, at the shelter. As cushy as that may seem, it was the last place that I wanted to be.

I would spend long hours with my crosswords books. When the office employees had taken their best shots at the newspaper puzzles, they would bring the unfinished ones to me.

At times I would have to consider that it was time to restart my functions in the real world: that is, the world beyond puzzle books. It was the emptiest of realities, but it was my own.

It was a time when the shelter itself wanted to get me involved at a higher level. I was given the position of weekend resident manager. "I'm honored!" I told them, but I respectfully declined. I told them that I had applied for a retail job which would require me to work weekends. The real situation was that I dreaded the contacts with other residents. It was clear to me that the counselors only recognized my energy, unselfishness, and intelligent day to day choices. They had not identified the harshness I endured just being in those dormitories. Nor had they recognized how I struggled to shut out the raw personalities that seemed to be getting closer with each hello.

I was holding up well as a resident-mate. I didn't want to find out where I would land if I became a resident authority figure. No! Just the idea of being held in higher esteem was a no-no for me.

One day I asked the volunteer cook if there was anything I could do to help out with the lunch hour. She was very pleased! She implied that she didn't trust the residents. She spoke as if she did not consider me a resident. As it happens, she had good reason to be wary. Her kitchen inventory had grown feet. Sometimes the supplies just walked away from their storage. She stayed only three hours each day. Those were three hours of distraction which I sorely needed.

XV-II

It was a distraction from the gibberish spun by my old buddy Jean. He had mentioned once that he appeared in a silent movie in 1938 and two more in 1939. As he spoke to us about his career, my only thoughts were whether or not to believe him. His age was appropriate with the period, however I did not know enough about the history of film making in New York to render an opinion. I would hear what he had to say then decide later if his stories could be valid. What I know about silent movies could fill a pillbox.

As time has gone by, and my friend has left the shelter, I have given some more consideration to his anxiety ridden claims. I have considered that it may be more than just talk. Having many innocuous hours, my consciousness has found a connection. It is quite possible that Jean was referring to a point in time when he was in California. My subtle knowledge of silent film history tells me that many studios existed in the outlying counties of New York City. Those were in full swing up to the late twenties. By the early thirties they had been transplanted to California. And as much as I tried to avoid dwelling on the possibility, Jean might have migrated to there as well.

When he was conversing, Jean kept his visions distant. That trait causes the listener's mind to wander a bit farther. It has the effect of enhancing a listener's experiences by drawing his own conclusions. For a time I worried that he only spoke to hear himself lie: the far-reaching experiences of which he spoke being only window dressing; stories spun for the purpose of finding an interested ear.

It is still possible however that those stories may be true. If so, it would be necessary for someone with his experiences to relate those stories in a distant manner. In other words, some parts should remain distant to avoid overwhelming the listener with obscured facts. The events would have occurred over such an extended period, and in such varied places as to make certain specifics irrelevant. In essence, the events are what is important. The how and the why of it all are left for the listener to decide.

Actually, the old guy is a rare being. He is one of a few people I've met who can speak to a broader aspect of the highways than can I.

For nearly three months now I have been ignoring friends and family, pretending not to know anyone, and laboring at the work center. How strange that I should point to someone else as being trapped in a routine of backbreaking work when I cannot get away from it. The other of my professional skills have been put on hold. My only requirement at this point in time, and my only source of comfort is to find another puzzle book.

On a different note, Jean's weightiness is not the only problem here. Another one is standing right in front of me. "Hey brother Al! Aint it wonderful to enjoy the lord's sunshine!"

"Yes sir Mr. Long! How are you today?"

"I'm a soldier! Amen! And a witness to his glory!"

"Yeah...well that's fine! I'm just about to go back to work! I mean, go pick up my work crew!"

"Brother Al, you can work and work to your heart's content. But you can never out-do what God has done. Praise him! That's why every morning when I arise, I know that I have arisen in heaven!"

"Amen Mr. Long! All I believe right now is that I need to get going!"

"That's it!" he said. "Don't you see? That's exactly why the book say's... 'Be not proud of thyself. In time you will be dust in the wind.'" "Yeah." I said. "Unless you want to pay my way, in time I will be kicked out of the shelter."

"Ha-ha-ha" he laughed. "A-a-a-ha-ha-ha-ha-men!"

XVII

Colleagues would not appreciate my use of the term 'lesser'. So in fact I will not speak of them in those terms. I will not even admit that my greatest fear at this place has been getting to be familiar. I dared not be party to their haplessness. For reasons which I have already made clear, I would not let myself reciprocate in friendships.

As I have discussed, they are a difficult constituency to live with. Everyone has good reasons for being here; yet I am not curious as to how each man ended up at this shelter. Still yet, I am not inclined to conduct interviews nor do a survey of my shelter mates. The best thing I can do for people like Big Bobby, Ivory, Bennie, and Mr. Long is to vanish. My best move is to get in he wind and hope it takes me a long way from here. When I break out the way Jean did, there will be no coming back. When I regain my stride, then and only then will I try to make some sense of this 'Divina Comedia'.

That description is right! This is a divine comedy of errors. It is one which I someday hope to look back on without consequence. I hope that all my hard work pays off. I can see myself in middle age being racked with pain. It may be worth it however just to survive this phase. I only know that, in order to dig myself out of this rut I must keep working. I must keep trying to improve my circumstances, while at the same time trying to not be overwhelmed by things happening in the world around me.

XVII-I

The face of our world will continue to change. Something totally unexpected may happen that could precipitate another setback for me. Though it seems unrelated, it could have something to do with current rumblings in the stock markets. Things are not going well.

But how will those matters affect my resurgence? I know not. I will have to give more thought to more things. I will need to determine with better intelligence what my options should be.

A devastating stock market crash would affect not just me, but everyone. The last great crash occurred in 1929. Virtually no one was spared disaster. Is there a chance that a similar event can happen?

Prior to that era, stock markets were something very different from today's worldwide brokerage. Earlier markets were helpful in promoting national causes and large manufacturing ventures. Investors bought stock as a way of supporting their nation. At the same time, a successful operation would bring financial rewards.

Markets in those times were more clearly defined. In Renaissance Europe for example, an investor could buy a share in support of expeditions to the new world. In so doing, he increased the monetary support behind that venture. His investment therefore made the odds of success more likely.

Another example of a clearly defined investment is someone who buys stock in a silkworm farm. Shareholders could follow the daily fortunes of their investment by getting up close and personal. They would not have to guess how the money is being used. Theirs was an operation which unfolded right before them.

Our modern stock markets are derived from the historical definitions of investment. But ours have mutated into something quite different. The term investment has taken on a new lexicon. The act itself is more accurately defined as speculating. Stock market investing has always been risky: many a cargo ship has been lost; and many textile plants have fallen victim to parasites. However, risks are what define twentieth century stock market investing.

Within this era our nation has been stricken with unprecedented growing pains. Just as it was recovering from a cataclysmic civil war, new manufacturing techniques propelled America into the industrial age.

Our government was experimenting with the post war Reconstruction Act. This was an imperfect attempt at mainstreaming former black slaves into the political system.

Inventors like Edison, Bell, and Ford were still ideating ways to use their patents. It was an era when ninety percent of the nation's money lay in the hands of less than five hundred people.

Oil and railroad barons controlled the nation's cash flow. Other than real estate, there was nothing pragmatically in which to invest. Nevertheless, people retained hope. The idea of becoming rich, spurred investment by the less fortunate. Thousands of companies prospered. Thousands more went bust.

This was an era when people invested not on venture, but on probability. Speculators could always believe in their dreams as they read the stock market journals. The reality is that those few who controlled the nation's wealth were not in the business of giving it away. Many citizens' hopes were crushed. An investor could wake up in the morning to great wealth. Then he might go to sleep that night completely broke.

Those were the days of the Model-T, flappers, and business monopolies. The average citizen was inured to hardships. He could anticipate everything from crop failures to being shot by strikebreakers. A man who had been uprooted from his life's work could only find his dream on the road.

In the course of uncharted fate, an energetic soul might have the urge to wander. Something inside tells him that if he travels the right path, greener pastures await. As a writer of that period once said; "...hope springs eternal in the human breast." It is a condition of human life. There is no way of stopping hope or motivation or one from accomplishing his goals.

An especially hard test of what lies inside the human spirit was the great stock market crash of 1929. The effects of which still resonate eighty years later. Surely it will resound throughout the ages.

This event changed the course of America's development. There were virtually no jobs. Men women and children stood on breadlines. Homelessness was a fact of life.

To view that era in hindsight some three generations later, it is easy to make assumptions about what actually happened. I believe this event to be an example of a thesis which I stated earlier. Those wealthy few were being plagued by envy of their status. Lower class citizens fervently desired to possess what they had.

Envy of their status certainly was a motivation for those extremely wealthy few to protect their worldly possessions. Paradoxically, our government viewed the rich as harmful. It was necessary for the government to impose antitrust laws. They made an effort to regulate the omnipotent stature of many businesses and their powerful owners.

Prior to the enactment of antitrust laws, large companies were allowed to buy out smaller less competitive ones. That practice could go on indefinitely until all competition was eliminated. Additionally, a large company could branch out into other related businesses. For example, a successful oil drilling company could legally own a refining company to process the crude. They could also own railroad companies to deliver the final product to market. The result was a conglomeration referred to as a Monopoly.

No small company could survive this kind of system. Certain individuals became so powerful, they could control the nation and its money. The raw practice of Capitalism was showing its final configuration. It was apparent that our system would soon become a dictatorship.

Our government moved wisely to legislate away those practices. They found the current practices to be cohabitant with he rise of large scale Monopolies. As with everything else that is run by a central government, Capitalism also requires legislative rules of engagement.

This is where, in my opinion the wealthy held their ground. They would not sit idly by and watch their system be legislated away. It was after all, how America became a world power.

I submit that powerbrokers of the day closed their ranks. They stood up in a way that showed the clout they had over the rest of our nation. I believe the crash of 1929 was the inevitable result. It was a real-time demonstration of the power which these men held. Involved as they were in a difficult tug-of- war with Congress, they simply pulled the rug from under our fledgling Capitalist base.

XVIII-I

Through many years of bank failures, starvation, joblessness, and other woes Americans became used to the hardships. Families sought ways to survive. Economic loss was a foregone conclusion. It was now time to maintain hope and faith in their abilities to carry on.

America became a nation of drifters. By rail, drawn wagons, car, or on foot, many people sought greener pastures. It would not have been out of the ordinary for a man to roam the continent. And because we know that people are well suited to roam and to rove, I can understand how a person might decide to hitchhike from the east coast of America, to the west coast.

The Great Depression was a time when my buddy Jean was a teenager. I would block those events from my mind if I could; but I cannot help dwelling on the problems which created him and many of our forerunners. When I am able to reconcile the history which Jean represented, maybe then his hardships won't seem so relevant. Probably if I did not have to hear the babble, his condition would not be of concern.

That being explained, I will consider the environment of an average depression era citizen. His story is one of loss, hardship, and peril. Yet there has to be some hope. There has to be some glimmer in the hearts of even these people.

From the stated experiences of some persons to whom I have spoken, I will tell a story of struggle and perseverance. For purposes of characterization and clarity, some of the names have been changed. I will revivify the heart of that darkest of times through the experiences of a boy named Tom.

XVIII-II

On a late summer morning in 1932, the sun rises on a large pauper colony. Young Tom and his family will have spent eight months there since being evicted from their New Jersey home. Neither he nor his father can find a job. His mother works four hours each day as a domestic servant. There are no set wages and she often accepts food instead of money. The work she does is barely enough to keep them fed. All through the harsh winter Tom has been dreaming of a better life. He thinks about the times when his family was much better off. They lived a very comfortable life. They were able to afford everything that they required. His father took care of the family in his capacity as an insurance broker.

Now there are no options for them. Even if the economy were to make a sudden reversal, it would still take years of struggle to re-establish the family business. Tom knows that his former life is over. He has come to the realization that the future of his family rests entirely upon his young shoulders.

He knows that the depression has affected every place along the east coast. No opportunities exist. Major cities in the mid-west are suffering as well. Once thriving stock yards, have no place to ship their product.

As if to put an exclamation point on the term suffering, mid-west farmers are experiencing the worst drought in their history. The region once green with crops is now called the dust bowl. Poor agricultural techniques had stripped the fertile top-soil of nutrients. Dust storms are forcing residents to leave their farms.

Tom made up his mind last December that it would be the last Christmas he'd ever spend in the colony. He felt in his heart that somewhere, somehow there is something more. He made up his mind that, that place is California. He had waited for this moment to arrive. And today is the day.

Before he sets out, Tom kisses his mother, and shakes his father's hand. He promises to come back for them. The heartbreaking moment was not what Tom's father had envisioned for his family. But now it had come. And then, Tom was gone.

The shadow of his parents hangs over Tom as he makes his way along the highways. He studied maps during the cold winter, to make his best route. He drew a line from the colony to Los Angeles. He wants to make his way as the crow flies. He had figured out the straightest and most direct plan.

Just outside his home state, Tom pulls the map from his pocket. He needs to reassure himself that he is in the right place. He had calculated that he would be able to hitchhike a ride to this Pennsylvania truck stop. It was early afternoon and things were going well. He felt invigorated and energetic. Now Tom rips apart his initial sign that said "Simmons' Truck Stop". He stares with pride at the sign that will take him to the land of opportunity: "California or Bust!"

No sooner had he held the sign aloft, did another trucker pull over. "Hello son. You got yourself quite a long distance to go!"

"Yes sir I do!" Tom said. "Can you help me out a ways?" "Why sure! Climb aboard!" The driver said. "I bet you're angling toward highway Sixty Six!"

"Yes sir!" Tom replied. "Is that where you're going?"

"Cleveland!" the driver said. "I'm taking supplies to the new construction sites over there. Lot's of work opening up right now; you might not have to travel so far after all!"

"I'm sure!" Tom said. "I've heard all about those new government projects.

Ole Roosevelt's going to make every man into a prince!"

"Maybe not a prince! But every man will have a job, or a way to make ends meet."

"I hope that comes true one day soon! The way things are right now, that work is going to men with families to support." said Tom. "How long do you think it would be before someone showed up with more experience and in more urgent need? In no time at all, I would be laid off and right back where I am now. Thank you for the information, but I think that I will do well on the other coast!"

"Well that's great my young friend. I admire your courage! And I wish you good luck!" "Thank you sir..." Tom responded.

After a few hours the truck driver spoke again. "Okay young man... this is your stop! This is Martin's Corner! You're about sixty miles north of Forty West. My guess is, you'll get another ride as soon as you hold that sign up!" "Thank you so much..." said Tom. "This is great! I appreciate it very much!" "You know...I'd bring you closer. But I would lose money on the load!"

Standing on the corner is part of the whole ordeal for Tom. But it has gotten dark, and he was getting cold. Thither by-ways, hither rain... nothing could dampen his resolve! As he stood there watching cars go by, he heard a voice call out to him. "No point in hurrying to where 'you're' going!"

"Yeah, you're right!" Tom responded "But I can't stay here!"

"Not true!" The man said extending his hand. "I'm Reverend Earl. I saw you with your sign over here! Thought I'd introduce myself. You see... we have a camp just over that embankment. It grew from people who would come to this intersection and do exactly what you are doing!"

"Try to catch a ride to Forty West?" Tom asked. "Yes!"... said the reverend... "Precisely!.. We have brethren who will be setting out in the next few days! We implore you to join us!"

"I thank you very much sir! I am rather tired! A warm tent sounds appealing right now."

It came as no surprise when Tom saw the sprawling camp. It consumed nearly four acres that he could see in the darkness. The tents were set in rows with enough room in between for all modes of traffic. Campfires lit up the community. He could see people moving about.

They all seemed to be at best comforted. From outside an archway, Tom could see the sign on the largest tent which read Salvation Army.

As Tom moved toward the gate he was greeted by a scruffy looking man who wore an old sailor's coat. "Halt who goes there!" the man said. "You dare try to enter without my permission?" Tom was startled, and surprised by the man's thick Irish accent. He stepped back quickly. The man continued to rant. "You're just a boy...and you think you can walk over me? Why, I ought to slit your damn throat!"

"I'm sorry!" Tom said. "Oh don't be afraid of him." Reverend Earl interjected. "That's old Murphy. He rarely ever get's out of that chair." "But why is he mad at me?" "He's not! He thinks he's still in the Great War. He was in the Royal Navy. His ship struck a mine and he lost a leg; obviously, he never fully recovered." "Oh... I see!" Tom said as he followed in through the gate.

The next morning, Tom felt refreshed. Finishing breakfast he watched the reverend climb atop a podium which held a small speaker's dais. Earl spoke in a loud voice to the crowd. He brought everyone up to date then spoke about their young visitor. He told them about Tom's effort to get away from the problems that had stricken most of the country.

"Finally..." he intoned "let us give our best wishes to this boy who has elected to seek out a better way! Rather than accept the conditions which have ruined us and many others, Tom has made it his goal to look for greener pastures. He has come to us all the way from the East Coast. But this is not the end for him." The Reverend paused and looked around. He waited until he had gotten everybody's attention, then he went on. "Nooo...!" he crooned. "This young man will not stop until he reaches California!" The crowd let out a gasp. Then there were some ooohs and aaahs. Then there was a loud round of applause.

"Our young man will need a lot of luck on his journey." the Reverend went on "But more than that he will need our prayers." He closed his eyes and reached skyward. "Oh Lord!" He said "Give this young man the strength and the endurance he will need to stay on the path. Oh Lord, give him the wisdom to recognize the dangers in these perilous highways. And give him the courage to escape all temptations he will meet along the way. Go with him Lord; guide him around every bend in the road! And most of all, Divine Savior; let him keep his dream alive!"

The audience stood and gave another round of applause. They joined the Reverend to sing an old gospel song... "We shall gather at the river! We shall gather at the river."

For Tom's purposes, the message was heart felt. His head was bowed as he thanked the reverend and shook his hand. Reverend Earl had in his grasp a piece of folded paper. He slipped it into Tom's hand as they shook. Tom unfolded the paper and saw that it was five dollars.

"Oh...no!" Tom said "please, you don't have to give me anything." "I know we don't" said the reverend "but we all want to see you succeed. Remember Tom, our hopes and prayers go with you!" "Thank you sir" Tom replied "I will. And god bless you all."

As Tom left the colony he was startled again by the old sailor. "Get back here ya salt!" old Murphy said. "Do ya think ya can escape from me? Well to hell with ya! To hell with you, your mother, and your father! All a ya's can kiss mi blimey arse!" "Yeah" Tom said under his breath "ya old fart!"

XIX-I

For more than a week, things have gone well for Tom. His travels across the states have been taxing, yet he finds himself enjoying the freedom. In his brief career as a hitchhiker, Tom has seen glittering peaks, and breadth taking valleys. As he made his way along highway forty he was stunned by the natural beauty. "Who could have made this?" he thought. "How divine god must be!" The sheer size of our nation has filled him with awe.

For the most part he has been riding. And there have been some brief periods of walking. They passed a sign that said "Welcome to Utah". Tom knew that the rules were about to change. Before that point, he was travelling from east to west. Soon he would have to make the transition from route forty, to route eighty in the south.

His present route would keep him north of his destination. He would end up in Oregon, or northern California. Tom wanted to be in southern California, at Los Angeles. According to his map, he needed to travel several hundred miles now in a north to south direction. He would eventually connect with route eighty. The easiest way to do that is from northern Utah to southern Arizona.

In his conversations with truckers they tended to agree with that. Long range drivers advised that he would have a difficult time if he continued over to the coastline. Most of it was still under development. His best turn over would be now. They told him about some highways that post-dated his map. It was not quite the thoroughfare that highway forty has been. This direction involved local roads, small towns, and snow covered mountain passes. Still it was his best connection with eighty.

And that's where Tom began his "Trek of a loftier kind". His sojourn along country roads took him to unfamiliar and sometimes scary places. Walking through Utah, the word "vertigo" came to his mind. The street winded up a mountain then around and down again. Tom began to swoon. His head spun as a downward plunge caused the blood to rush from his feet to his eyes.

Tom wore a sign which said "Eighty or bust" as he stayed to the right. Automobile traffic was sparse. He could walk for hours and not hear a motor. But he felt great.

The signs which Tom wore, that had solicited so much excitement last week, were not so far-fetched at this location. Tom was getting closer to his dream. He has come a long and diverse way. The excitement in the air now was felt by Tom. It put more quickness in his step. Staring at his new surroundings Tom could sense the optimism that used to be hidden within his soul. The skies seemed bluer, and the atmosphere smelled more pristine. "There's no depression around here!" he thought to himself.

XIX-II

Now and then Tom would see some folk travelling in horse drawn wagons. This was his mode of travel for several days. The locals got a big thrill from hearing about Tom's life back in New Jersey. They thought it really bazaar that the industrialized, highly developed east coast has found itself in such a tumultuous state. Tom learned that agriculture was thriving in their part of the world. The great drought of the mid-west did not affect them at all. He became aware that industrialization played a very small role in this part of the world too. These gentle folk were almost oblivious to oil magnates, Wall Street brokers, and anything remotely related to a stock market crash.

Word was spreading about the young hitchhiker. As he made his way to Nevada, and to northern Arizona the local folk started to take part in his voyage. Sometimes people met him along the highway to provide a meal. Other times they would give him fresh clothes and a place to bathe. Tom saw a boy who told him that the biggest news on telegraph wires was about him.

People were moved by, his story. They were curious about him and about what could set him off on such a pilgrimage. Everybody wanted to help out in some way.

Tom finally got into Arizona. The landscape changed very rapidly. Rocky heights now turned into desert valleys. He walked easily along. As he studied the rock mesa formations above the desert floor, he studied his gait below. He envied his stride as he moved along. The sound of an automobile echoing through the canyons caused his left thumb to go up. A voiced called to him. "Hey Tom!" the driver said. "How are you today?"

It was totally unexpected. Tom glanced at the man, realizing that he was a complete stranger. "I'm fine sir!" He replied. "How are you?" "Just fine, young man: Just fine." Tom knew that he was a celebrity around this area so the surprised look on his face soon turned to excitement. "I'm Kevin Ackerman. I sell pots and other wares along these highways." "Well hello Mr. Ackerman! I'm pleased to make your acquaintance."

The echo of a motor in the canyon made Tom raise his thumb.

"I was visiting the Williams family yesterday. They told me all about you!" "Yes," Tom said, looking into the car window. "the Williams; they invited me to dinner a few days ago. They're very nice people."

"Well Tom," said Ackerman, "you won't believe where I'm going to next." "Where?" said Tom. "I'm going all the way to highway eighty!" "Fabulous!" shouted Tom as he opened the front door. "Just put your bags in front Tom. You get in the back. I hear you've been walking since five o'clock this morning." "That's right Tom replied." "That's almost seven hours." Ackerman said. "You stretch out on the back seat. I'll be making a few stops along the way. You might get about five hours of sleep until we get to your road." "Hey, thanks Mr. Ackerman! I really appreciate your kindness." "It's not a problem my young friend! I'm glad to have this chance to help out."

The car wheezed and lurched! The tumbling transmission soon smoothed itself out as the automobile got up to speed. "Nice Oldsmobile!" said Tom, as they cruised along. "Thank you! It's been very dependable! We can use a few new parts of course. But; so far, so good!" Tom laughed and dozed off to sleep.

The rickety car settled into a low pitched rhythm. The beat reminded him of a poem that he had learned in grade school. As he drifted into dreamland, he could remember the poem: but the words were a little bit different now.

OUR STREET

THERE WAS A STREET I CALLED MY OWN!
SULTRY LANES, AND PATHS WHERE YOUTH HELD SWAY.
LANGUISHING BEAMS MOVED US ALONG.
YES THERE WAS A STREET BACK IN THE DAY.

AND THERE WAS AN ADDRESS I CALLED HOME!
THERE ON OUR BLOCK, REGAL AND GAY.
KIDS VOICES ECHOED THROUGH PAVED COMBS
INFECTING THE YEARS THAT SHAPED OUR PLAY.

AND I KNOW A WAY TO GO BACK THERE!
STRAIGHT! LIKE AN ARROW GUIDING MY WAY,
TO UNCHECKED FAUNA AND BALMY AIR.
DREAMS TAKE ME BACK; WHERE I USED TO STAY.

The blast from a truck horn caused Tom to sit up. He saw Mr. Ackerman stir, then wake up. "Where are we?" he said. "Good morning Tom!" said Ackerman yawning and sitting up from his front seat bed. "We're on highway eighty, at the High Desert Truck Stop."

"Oh!" said Tom "Was I asleep very long?" "I would say so..." answered Ackerman "It's after three in the morning." "Okay..." said Tom pausing briefly to gather himself. "So, where do you go from this place?" "Well, I'm going to sleep for a few more hours. Then at around six in the morning, I'll start to make my way east; toward Phoenix." "Okay Mr. Ackerman. I'll give you a stir after sunrise."

Three hours later, Tom shook Ackerman. "Hey... it's about that time sir! You slept very soundly." "I sure did son! I feel much better now... Looks like a nice day to peddle some wares." "Yes it's a very nice day" Tom replied. "Did you make many sales while I was asleep?" "No Tom. Things didn't go as I'd hoped. But it's a new day; maybe they'll pick up!"

"You deserve better Mr. Ackerman. You turned a five day walk for me into a pleasant eight hour ride. I have something for you sir." Tom reached into the lining of his coat. He unpinned the folded piece of paper that Reverend Earl had given to him. Mr. Ackerman watched as Tom peeled off three dollars.

"This money has been a test for me Mr. Ackerman. I realize now that God gave it to me to give to you. I have been at a crossroads for many months now. Over the last few days I learned that there is a lot of good in a lot of people."

"Thank you Tom." Replied Ackerman humbly. "I would refuse this if I dared: truth is, I came to this truck stop to barter for some gasoline. This money will fill my tank." Ackerman lowered his head for a moment and nodded at the money. Then he spoke to Tom again. "It takes a smart young man to know what this means to a travelling salesman. I know you'll do well in California." "No thanks needed sir! I finally got the chance to help someone."

They shook hands and wished each other good luck. Ackerman had some more advice for Tom before they went their separate ways. "Ya know Tom, I used to live in Los Angeles!" he confided. "The situation there is becoming more and more cut-throat, but I finally was able to break into the business. They thought that I had great potential as an actor. I worked hard; made all the right connections. I took some bit parts. And I even read a couple of times for co-starring roles. I was flying high. It seemed as though nothing would bring me down. But something was wrong with my choices." "Oh no!" said Tom. "What was it?" "Fame!" said Ackerman. "I'm not meant to be a celebrity."

"As a bit player getting just the taste of fame, it put a bad taste in my mouth. The only thing I had to do was to smile and wave at the fans. But I couldn't do that. For some reason I don't know, the crowds were not what I wanted. They would reach out to shake my hand, and I would push them away. When they handed pictures to me for an autograph, I would throw them aside. Whatever you do out there Tom, remember that it's all in your mind. You decide who you are, and you stick with that. The only stars in this universe are the ones set by God in heaven.

XIX-VI

And thus ends our tale of the boy hitchhiker: a story related by this writer to bring clarity to the matter of being a drifter. Tom is a fictional character. His tribulations and his accomplishments are real. They are a part of life for more people than I previously believed. Looking at the situation from Tom's point of view has helped me to understand a lot more. He began his quest with a single purpose. His experiences, his qualities, and his surroundings propelled him across thousands of miles. To know what Tom achieved is to know how something that seems impossible can be possible. The presentation of this story is what is needed to explicate some questions about the drifter.

Tom was pressed into attempting the impossible. He was doomed if he didn't and damned if he did. Unbridled hope compelled him to take the big chance.

Revelation of those deeds also helped to answer tricky questions. There was the question of support systems. Are there drifter support systems in America? The answer we have seen is yes! So now the issue becomes; how does a teenager with no skills in hitchhiking travel from coast to coast in safety and with comparative ease?

Our characters answer this question with their amity. Even though fate had put Tom in one of the most difficult situations imaginable, he was gifted in the most important regard. Everybody he encountered did their best to help out. They all identified with the boy's effort to recourse his life. They also recognized what he was up against.

The "poor man's society" in which Tom travelled knew that desperate times, called for desperate measures. Tom was a product of those times. A victim of profiteers gone haywire.

His journey was made tolerable by an admiring constituency. People whom he never met before took him under wing. They wanted Tom to realize his dream. And in so doing, strike a blow for every person who felt the sting of the Great Depression. To their imperiled society, Tom was the promise of a new beginning. He represented durability, sincerity, and hope which always springs eternal.

The other question is; what on God's earth makes the trek a way of life?

What kind of background does one need to live his life as a wanderer?

Events that unfolded in Tom's life have shown that there is no experience needed. For this youth, there is no beginning, and there is no end! He is further proof that humans have an innate trait which facilitates movement across long distances. In addition to our physiology which keeps us upright and forward looking, we have the ability reach out when someone is in need. We can share another person's burden, even if that person is a stranger. He is a member of the family of man.

Especially in times of strife, we recognize that glory comes from our togetherness. We are empathetic to the trials of others. We can make a case for good, and for bad. Tom did not pose a threat to the people he met. It was evident to those people that he was making a sincere effort to perpetuate his journey. They took into consideration Tom's strongest asset, his focus on the destination. Tom was doing what comes natural. He rationalized a goal; he planned its course, and he set out to achieve its end. The admiration society which he encountered only served to invigorate his steps. It may well be that the most rigorous part of Tom's goal, was travelling there.

It is very difficult to thrive in a strange city. The problems in doing so are magnified when there are no friends or family to help out. Things would be easier for young Tom if he knew that there was someone to turn to in California. Going it alone is like "just passing through..." nothing is given! Tom cannot be certain if he will find a means of support, or if he will be left in the cold.

A newcomer to unfamiliar territory has to investigate every avenue. Failure at early opportunities should not mean that the game is over. It should count as experience for the next opportunity. One has to be diligent. Remain confident at all times. And one must never quit.

It is easy to be cynical when things are not going well. To have an "untoward mentality" is a flaw. When your outlook on a new opportunity is the same as your outlook on the last, you exude the aura of expecting to be turned away.

There will be some anxiety. And there has to be some anticipation. Each new venture is a new chance. Having failed before, should not be grounds for repeated failure.

The major reason for being in a new environment is to start over. One's first priority then is to be at a favorable starting point. Though it is a difficult proposition if he does not know the landscape, one eventually will find his niche. He must remain comfortable and confident. This will be an attribute which appeals to prospective careers.

Confidence is a component that can spread to others. It can influence those you contact. It can affect the way that others look at you!

There is a pace to life. Our young hitchhiker is the perfect example of when to establish a tempo. Move too fast, and run the risk of throwing away energy that is replenished in the body. Move too slowly, and possibly miss the opportunity of a lifetime. One should not wait for a good break to happen. He should pursue whatever favors that are out there to be gained.

Don't put all your eggs in one basket. A big mishap will cause all of them to break. It is better to bring a few samples to the table; investigate your options, then come back with more eggs. To present a well-made product is a strong attribute. Whether we are talking about eggs, or about personal image, there must be an air of confidence.

One's ability to move forward with an air of confidence is an indication that he can achieve what he sets out to do. Ironically, the more you try, the more experienced you become. If one see's those attempts as fruitless steps, he will lose confidence. Therefore one should view each effort as a learning experience.

With time, the stranger can become focused on his setting. He can see more clearly where he is going, and what to expect when he gets there. He is near accomplishing his goal of leaving the past behind.

There is nothing in the way of experience to facilitate my understanding of residents on the the yard. With the exception of Bennie, I have never seen any one of them before. When I gazed at someone, I could only see their circumstances. There seemed to be virtually nothing to say. I could not ask how they were doing. The environment spoke for itself. Eye contact was brief. I did not know them well enough for sustained conversation.

There was very little subject matter to discuss. If so; it involved topics like how to operate the laundro-mat. Or where to get a new bar of soap; or where to get donated clothing. It was my first exposure to the matter of wearing used clothing. Eventually I had to give in to the situation. The clothes which I already possessed were not suitable for wearing to the work center. Ultimately, I was in the wrong place at the wrong time. I could not be selective. All I could do was go with the flow.

I would never stoop so low as to drink a cup of beer that was left on a park bench. Walking in the path of this group exposed me to that episode. It made me feel dejected. Others laughed. Humor is not a strong suit of mine.

I would ease the tension by pretending to understand. However, that venue felt out of place. There was nothing to be gained by laughing all the time. I stopped listening to Jean's bull-dash. He seemed now to be the smartest of example of these others. He is a man who survived those infinite experiences of which he speaks, to end up here.

These comrades presume to be unsophisticated. They do not spin to cultural effects. They are their own clowns. They assume that everyone in their presence is unsophisticated. They would rather be in the presence of this kind of person. My behavior has potential, but for the most part I am not who they prefer. You may view me as hostile company.

On some occasions I have have been seen playing the game. I have pretended to be someone "in the know". On each of those occasions

I was hiding behind Jean. I was in with the gibberish because Jean always injected himself into the goings on. My assumption that he did not relish in this was proven to have been wrong. In fact, he thrived on it.

I believed at first that there was some social science being applied. I was looking for something scholarly in his manner. It appears, to my dismay that he is the same as they. This group provides a "comfort zone" with which Jean is wholly familiar. He apparently would not have it any other way.

For my part, there is no compromise. I was not attuned to their capacities when I came here: and I will not have aquired them when I leave. Being able to recognize Jean's assimilation only spurred my urgency in getting out. I began thinking that I had to move soon.

I must at this stage, consider all types of issues. I must look at issues which pertain not just to me, but to other people. We all have our individual choices to make. Each person has a different way of doing things. Everyone has a certain level of stress and urgency.

These times are unlike those when I absolutely, positively knew who I was. I had envisioned a goal; and I was moving patiently towards it. These times now seem to be for re-coursing. It's clear to me. From the location that I am in right now, there is no more important time to reconfigure my aims.

I can see clearly that windows are closing. Some opportunities are less available. I feel less capable of doing what I thought I should do. This milieu was quicksand. I knew that I had to regain my status. I needed more solid footing. Whenever someone is facing conditions of undue stress, there is someone else who cares. One may not recognize that others desire to help, but society has proven time and again that it does.

In my ongoing situation at the shelter, I could not have imagined how caring and empathy would help me. For many weeks now, I have felt that I was in a steel trap. I had come to the worst of all possible conclusions. It was not until I came to the point of transitioning out of the place that I felt my way being eased.

It was at a point when my brooding stopped and I had found a full-time job. I hold many professional licenses. I am certified in education, journalism, law enforcement, I have been a guidance counselor, and in retail management. At this point however I was not pursuing any of the above positions. I settled for a job in security. All I had to do was sit there all night with my radio close by. Every hour or so, I made my rounds.

Security was something I had done briefly in my college years. Each summer, a few of my basketball teammates and I remained in-state. Our coach had a friend who owned a security company. It paid our room and board. On our free time, we worked out in the gym. Those years became a valuable reference for getting the job that I recently landed.

XX-III

A big advantage of living around so many other males is that you will find an auto mechanic. Some of them made it possible for me to obtain a car. I hadn't enough money to invest in a good used car. But I needed one in the worst way. A resident said that he had a solid chassis and body that he would let me have for one hundred dollars. His stipulation however was that the car did not run. A buddy helped me tow it to his son's house. He lived down the street from "Auto Graveyard". We repaired some parts and replaced some too. By nightfall the car was in perfect running condition. It was a god-send. Things could not have worked out better.

My work shift began at midnight. The last bus to the worksite was at ten o'clock. Before I got the car I would arrive two hours early, and hang out. The job became a legitimate way for me to clean up my act.

XX-IV

Nevertheless, those psychopathic elements in the dorm still found a way to manifest themselves. There were always some men who could not identify with my need to work constantly. They came up with a way to antagonize my efforts at every step.

Every morning when I came back from work, I went to bed. Most of the men would go outside and about their ways. A few others would bring the gibberish back inside. They lounged around the hallways talking in very loud voices. I could not sleep. When I dozed off, someone would shake my bed. I would wake up in time to see a man running down the hallway.

I don't know if I was their only target, but it sure felt that way. There was an element in the group who still pictured me as being too different. I had been around them long enough to understand the prevalent psychology. Yet I could not wrap my brain around this particular shortfall. The tendency was to not only disapprove of my achievements; they were antithetical to success. I realized there was nothing I could do. I dare not ask them to get out. I just lay there counting the number of paychecks I needed to get a new apartment.

After about a week, dorm counselors called a meeting of all residents. They set new rules for the dormitories. To my surprise, they established that no one could re-enter the dorms after breakfast hours. The hallways would remain empty until four o'clock in the afternoons.

Only those residents who worked the previous nights would be allowed inside. Violation of the rules would result in immediate eviction.

I stood and said thank you. For the first time in two weeks my head was not spinning. It appears that someone cared enough to report the situation. Those men who could not understand why I needed my space, simply disappeared. They were legislated out of existence. Yet their motives trouble me to this day.

I often wonder about this particular feature in human beings. I often wonder to what extent this dark heartedness has impeded our development. I also have wondered what creates this sort of demonic fervor. For someone to hear about it is nerve wrecking. To have been caught up in it is torture.

Is it immaturity? In a group of children... maybe! But in a group of adult males it is something much deeper.

I sought a more analytical view of the issue. In order to help myself understand, I wanted to reconnoiter, and be very thorough. As things stood, it may be said I only imagined the anguish because of where I was. But I think there is more to it. It is a pervasive condition.

It happens in the 'Blue Light Districts' of Netherlands, in opium dens of Hong Kong, and with child prostitutes in Thailand. It happened in German death camps, as well as in megalopolises of India. It pervaded the shanty towns of Brazil; and the fringe cities of Mexico. My list goes on: from expansionist America, to the Australian Outback; from terrorist training camps in the middle east, to the mid-twentieth century, Empire of Japan.

It is not a counter-command to people's ability to care for each other. It is an entirely different side of man. As much as we admired the story of Tom, the young hitchhiker, we know that our most famous hitchhikers are serial killers. They are a one-in-a-million type of hitchhiker, but they do exist. They also, are functioning definitions of dark heartedness.

My up-close experience has awakened me. Certainly, none of my siblings behaved that way. My classmates and neighborhood kids never exhibited a cruel mindset. Everyone whom I recall, was pleasant. There were a few bullies. I avoided them throughout my life. Now it appears that they are unavoidable. They are a group that fits perfectly into my psycho analytic formula. This formula is one that I developed in an effort to clearly understand the behavior that I witnessed. My resulting formula equates to those persons who are: 2 sensuous 2 have used any 4 thought. They do what they actually feel. Often-times, the feeling is of a dark nature.

The word sensuous may not be cross referenced in my formula with the word sensual. They stem from the same root; the word "sense". Yet, these words are now divergent. In my equation they cannot be interchanged. They even sound similar in meaning: 'Sensual'- Of the body or the senses, as distinguished from the intellect: 'Sensuous'- Of, perceived, or enjoying sensation absent of intellect.

My formula identifies a status in humans where the sensuous urges outweigh the need for intellectual inducement. It is when a person enjoys what he is feeling to the extent that he is loath to think about a reason for it. The feeling is so deeply rooted in 'sensuousness' that it overrules thought and imagination. In this state, a person will chomp down on the feeling. He refuses to think about his condition: "... lest it be reasoned away". The resulting behavior depicts how someone can actually be mindless.

This condition is not restricted to time. Sensuousness can last a few minutes, or it might consume a lifetime.

Man's greatest weapon is his intellect. He lacks fangs, and has no claws. He cannot run down an elk. He cannot jump up and catch a bird. Man cannot ingest ninety percent of the earth's vegetation. His greatest option is his brain. In order to survive he has to outsmart other carnivores. He has to isolate those vegetables that he can eat, and proceed to outsmart nature.

Man is the only creature with the wisdom to plant a garden. No other earthly thing can place seeds into the ground, and wait for them to blossom. Human beings, in fact have to be intellectual to survive.

So why do we have all the sensuousness? Ironically, those persons who exist within my formula are doing so at the expense of their fellow man. If they are too hooked on a feeling to care about others, consequently some other person must care for them. Those who exhibit shortcomings of intelligence cannot survive this harsh, unfriendly environment. Other people have to care enough about them to pick up the slack.

So what happens when an entire society fits into the formula of dark heartedness? Then, it is up to other societies to rise above them. Man has been known to utilize the dark hearted side in order to facilitate ambitions. They program their souls in a way that serves their plans. They work off of any necessary feelings which spread their ideology.

When successful, they turn into a kind of idealized snake, weaving its way through city and country. Exposing its fangs; basking in recognition, and letting everyone know that..."we are who we are! We refuse to change our dark hearted intent. We feel good, and we love being this way!"

XX-VII

Because they cannot see the bigger picture, those persons in my formula only deal with what lies in front of them. They acquire the necessities in life by tapping others: even if it means, acquiring things dishonestly.

This infers that groups which practice dishonest ideals enjoy what they are doing. In my equation, they maintain a sort of sensuous happiness. They lurk in a gray area of invisibility. And they can feel that their ways are successful.

Those persons who do things the honest way must look for an occasional handout. When successful they are content and happy. Until; that is, they need another handout. By visiting their dark hearted ways upon me, those residents at the dorm, showed that pain and hurt are an ever present component. They imagined me as someone being dismissive of their feelings. My tendency to keep separation between us only built mistrust. Further, I spurred envy when I landed the security job.

I was on the verge of busting out of this oppressive subculture. I proved that I could withstand society's hidden pitfalls and pull myself up from the rut. All it took was hard work and self respect.

But it seems the men in that environment were not ready to applaud my achievements. Their interests lay more in keeping me subjugated at that place. They continued to make fun of my car, of me working in the rain, and about me doing other people's chores.

It is probable that they have never seen anyone by his own devices lift himself up and out of their condition. It only goes to prove what I thought all along. Someone with my kind of optimism did not belong in that kind of place. And homeless does not equate to hopeless.

In the end I set neither good nor bad examples for my brethren. I faced my biggest fears, and have reconciled myself with their effects. I must continue to work hard as a way of avoiding ruin. And I cannot let my life be derailed by the ignorance of others.

As odd as it may seem, I have only gratitude for the facility itself. After all it beats the hell out of sleeping on a park bench. I learned to respect the stiff rules. Having been there a couple of months, I can relate to their importance. There is no etiquette but for those imposed by the shelter. There are issues of hygiene. Clothes must be washed and beds made. There is a curfew to be observed; no one gets in afterwards.

Things which I took for granted, had to be forced upon most of the residents. I would go into more detail if I had the desire. However, I have been explicit enough thus far to be clear.

XI-IX

I was avoiding the counselors at this point in my stay. It was not in a way of animosity. I simply was looking forward to rinsing my thoughts of this entire episode. They were aware that I would not take any assistance or benefit packages. They were reluctant to discuss the existence of any program that might help my cause.

When we communicated, we spoke as peers. They had some information that could help me immensely. Their challenge was to catch me with my guard down. They might penetrate my ego, and propose a quick way out.

One day I was in the office of our lead counselor. He was telling me about a career opportunity he would take in D.C. The conversation eventually drifted to apartment availability. It led to a program for which I was eligible. Persons who had been here for approximately the time that I had, were were encouraged to find their own place. Part of that encouragement included financial help. He told me about the donor's bank which would pay half my first month's rent and deposit.

"Take it Al..." he said. "...You've done so much for morale here! We're all cheering for you." At that very moment, I became a recipient. My pride said "no", but my common sense said "Thank you".

I walked back through the hallways staring at the floor. That conversation certainly had put some pep in my step.

The one thing about my locker which antagonized me was that it was adjacent to Mr. Long's bed. As I walked by, he extended his hand. "Be at at peace with this situation!" he said. "Your fruit will bear in their season."

"Thank you Mr. Long." I replied. "I'll remember that."

XXI-I

People can be very pretentious when they want to. There is so much hypocrisy inside us. To think that some from my past would be concerned with reputation. It is really beyond me. Yet I had to be cautious.

Part of the reason that I felt dumfounded was due to anger. It was anger for those who would be my judge. I had never before let that emotion dwell in my circles. But earlier in this year, circumstances began to overwhelm me.

I was angry that no one returned home when my parents got sick. I was angry that I was the only sibling who felt the need to move back in with them. And finally, when my older sister inherited our childhood home, I was blown away that she remortgaged the property.

At some point in this comedy I began to struggle with the feeling of being shoved under. I was unable to think about the blossoming career that I left up north. And I could not see where I fit in down here.

Now that I have survived a rite of passage at the shelter, I am ready to move away and beyond into my new apartment. I hoped to re-establish contact with my family. I could not verbalize what I really expected from them. As it happened, they could not have been more distant. In the year before, they didn't appear to share the sadness I had over the loss of our parents. They even went so far as to recommend that I see a doctor. I admit to being grief stricken. Still, the events had more life changing effects on my siblings than on me. I would not take part in the drama over who gets what. I told them to divide my share.

There are many things different in our relationships this time around. We still are, and always will be family. There is however, a different standard which has left me uncommitted to to appease them. I will never turn my back on them. I simply refuse to indulge them. They must learn to respect my space.

I have issues that need to be addressed, which only time can accommodate. They involve some brethren who also took advantage of the program that I'm on. Every so often a few of them would stop by. Unfortunately, these former shelter mates view me as one of their own.

Our conversations always revolved around ways to beat the system. They are very creative along those lines. Even though governmental assistance helps them with every phase of their lives, they constantly search for ways to get more.

They were eager to cite Mr. Long as the perfect example. They believe Mr. Long got over like "...a fat rat." He was eventually classified by the State as a mental disability. He gets a monthly check, and he lives in a three bedroom house on the west side. Everyone fell into uncontrollable laughter when Sparks told us about the circumstances; "...he said the lord blessed him as mental!" They rolled around laughing until I told them that I was expecting family.

It took some convincing, but I finally got them to understand that I was paying everything out of my own pockets. I chose to live uptown; not because assistance was available, but because it is the way of life for me.

I knew that the guys were somewhere laughing at me. It's just the way that they are. The important thing was that they had stopped coming to my house. They must know by now that I take no pleasure in ridiculing others. They should have understood that I was not amused by what they had to say about Mr. Long. I admired the way he stuck to his beliefs. I think he got what he deserved. I know that his faith is what got him there. In any case he is smarter and more likeable than those others. I can only hope that his location does not cause him to waiver. A lot of the west side where he was sent, are breeding grounds for men and women at the shelter.

XXII

Where have those gentle breezes gone? Where are those soft winds that embraced and guided me through my existence? Where is the atmosphere that held my world together? Things are not the same. Days and nights are spent wrapped in pensive thought. I stare at the walls until they close in on me. I have yet to draw any dynamic conclusions.

There was a time when delightful raw urges wafted through my brain. I had things to do, places to go, and people to see. I would make my presence felt. There were moves to make and stories to tell. Nowadays I don't have a need.

Family is still important, but they are not as close fitting. There was a time when everyone came home for the holidays: Spring Break, Summer Break, and Christmas. Any occasion that prompted extended travel time, was a chance to come home.

I recall how I used to arrive home a week or so early for Christmas. I helped my mother put up the traditional decorations. Sometimes one of my older brothers would come in early. They wanted to be out of town, and back up north before Christmas day. As soon as they arrived the tussling would follow. My sister-in-law would start to dismantle the decorations. She was always in disagreement with what we had done. One year I remember especially, I got so upset I was ready to move to a hotel until they left. She had my nephew Kevin climb a two story fern tree in our front yard, and take down the the tree lights.

She preferred them to be strung in a circular pattern rather than straight up the tree trunk as I had done. I watched from the living room window, hoping that he would fall off the ladder.

To avoid a fight, I went along with their input. After all, it was Christmas.

They are family! And I had not been singled out to decorate the house.

XXII-II

Still, those days are filled with color. It is difficult now even to regress and think fondly on them. Things have changed so quickly. The one redeeming factor is that I have been down this road before. I can say that there is an aura of deja vous. I think that I can deal with these matters.

If and when I need to reach out to someone, I know that I can give Pia a call. I'm sure that she will still talk to me. When I left my job up north I also left her. She knows however that I have great love for her. That has been our understanding. We have great love for each other. If only it hadn't been so long. Things would certainly have been different.

I have, as a consequence seen myself on an alternative path. I would look at other perspectives and have different priorities. Though my identity would be the same, I would look for different distractions. I would be in a way that requires me to share my optimism with others. At a time when I am most confident about my inner strength, I can see myself sharing it with others.

There is a new path that beckons me. It calls and waits and urges. It is eager to judge the new me. It looks forward to the chance to put me to the test: to examine all the changes; real and imagined.

Have I twisted fate? Have I triumphed in an age old rite of self determination? The past year has been a perfect collaboration of some of my greatest fears. Yet I survived. Herein is the onset of deja vous. I have a strong feeling that I will survive this too. I have been trampled, only to rise up and get past it all. The challenge now facing me is to determine what avenues are important.

I could bail out, the way my old buddy Jean did. I would just go away for no apparent reason. I would leave everybody guessing where I went. To do that however, is not very likely of me. At all times in the past when I uprooted, everyone knew where I was going. I prepared meticulously so as to insure a certain quality of life. I left no questions in my wake. Nor did I leave the impression that I would never come back.

If I had known that Jean was hitting the road again, I would not have tried to stop him. The way that he left was his usual means of doing things. There were no fond goodbyes. They only imply some kind of attachment. We know that attachments are not smiled upon in drifter parlances. That is why his conversations were so spaced out. He represents the appearance of comradeship. His existence is so spaced out, that he could have ended up at any place in the polite drifter world.

Once in a conversation with him, Jean told me that he knew everything there is to know about Savannah. He said that he had lived in this city before. Knowing his propensity for storytelling, I asked him "when" it was that he lived here. He responded..."fifty years ago!"

I have great admiration for Jean's intelligence. But I will not confer upon him any qualities of common sense. His spaced out ways tell me that he will never find a stable location in his life. Therefore, I hereby confer upon him the title of "Drifter Scholar."

I can see more clearly now where I must be, and with more certainty how to get there. Only a perfect upbringing could have prepared me to overcome this detour. There is a slight chance that I could have gone with the path of my brethren. I could have settled for a more simplistic lifestyle.

This county is filled with low-rent domiciles. I could be living in a room at the end of a long hallway. I would do soft work occasionally to pay the twenty five dollars per month's assisted rent.

I would not worry about food. There are many food banks and eateries that I could have access to. They would meet all of my needs.

I would not struggle to keep my car running. I wouldn't have a car. I would have a bus pass. I could go anywhere the bus route takes me. Or, better yet I could ride my bicycle. I would go wherever I pleased. It would be paradise; like a Greek island. No license plate fees. No insurance fees. No sticker fees. Yes, the easy life. I can see myself there. Ever to be eased: television my constant companion.

However, that is not how it turned out. I know that I cannot live under those circumstances. The easier life is, the more troubled I become. I require the scrutiny of a challenge. I need to be pushed, in order to be viable. The hectic way of life presses upon my brain. It keeps me advancing forward. For whatever reason; social or genetic, I must triumph over my surroundings.

These lessons are some which I learned early in life. They are the ones that guide me today. They are constantly recreated and revisited in my mind. Sometimes I see them in my daily thoughts. Sometimes they are in my deepest dreams.

I will describe in detail one of those dreams. Thereby you the reader can better understand the sequence of events being revealed. In fear of the almighty, this is how things unfolded.

XXIII

Once I beheld an enlightened dream. It occurred about a week after I graduated college. I was in my early teens when the basis for it took shape. It alluded to parallels between all beings that walk the earth. All things that are born to be motile have to express motility. It is the law of our universe. They are obligated to move from point 'A' to point 'B'. What came to me was a masterpiece of the psyche. These were images of God's creatures doing what their instincts told them to do. All creatures are guided by their diverse and eternal abilities. My subconscious was attempting to decipher why they did so.

In the distance there was a boy calling. He ran to my house and said to me "There are deer on the parkway!" We ran two blocks down the street to catch a glimpse. But they had already gone. The parkway was a nearly completed state project. It is a massive six-lane highway that connects to some other interstates in the region. It was no longer the huge mound of red clay that we had known. It would soon be ready for automobile traffic.

A few years later while I was home for spring break, I had the opportunity to drive along the parkway. I accepted it as progress, even though I did not like the way it obliterated the landscape. It slammed through many neighborhoods; strode across some area rivers, and terminated several local roads. As I took in the way it cut out much of the forest land, it brought back the incident from long ago when we ran to see the deer on the parkway.

Later that year as I lay in bed asleep, I was overcome with an amazing vision. I saw myself kneeling at the bedroom window, watching cars go down the parkway. That's when I saw what appeared to be a herd of deer. They plodded slowly along. Some stopped occasionally to graze on the tall grass in the median or on the shoulders. They would immediately join the others and continue on. Throughout the moonlit night I watched. Hours went by. I was awestruck by this amazing sight.

As I lay in bed staring through the window, I could see that they were still on the move. Days, then weeks went by. The herd did not relent. After some months I began to think that it would always be this way. The herd of deer would never end. Automobiles would never again use the parkway.

Unimpeded they continued forward. I could walk to the corner and see them trampling by. It no longer seemed like an event. It seemed only natural.

By autumn, I imagined that the herd covered every adjoining interstate system. I continued to watch, though I had become used to them plodding along. They chewed on the falling leaves which dotted their path. I could only guess at which highways the lead deer had taken. I was in no position to be deductive after all, it was only a dream.

My only option was to wake up. But I did not. I lay there and watched. Amazingly, the baby deer and the fawn were high-stepping alongside the adults. On and on they went.

Gradually, I could see a slight change in the condition of the animals. The ones in this phase of the herd were a little thinner. Though it did not matter to them, this part of the herd was of lower priority than earlier ones. They appeared to be in less than premium condition. This could be attributed to the veracious eating habits of the others. For whatever reasons, their venture was more of a struggle.

Still, on they trod. Fewer abreast, and searching farther away from the middle path, they found their way. They were constituents of the herd. One path, one impulse, one heard, they went on.

When I sat up in my bed, I thought that the vigil was over. When I fell back into blissful sleep, they were still on the move. Sparser in number, this latter group defined their segment of the herd.

Well into the winter months they controlled the parkway. They beat at the soil with their hooves. I saw that one of them would find an occasional root or buried twig. It was a time of blight. They did not have many choices. Vegetation was little and far between. The animals spread out as they advanced. They darted in and out of neighborhoods, searching for sustenance. They overturned garbage cans and hopped into dumpsters. They were barely tolerating the direst of conditions. By the time they left, virtually nothing remained. The ones that followed this segment were certainly at their wit's end. Their very survival was in question.

Ultimately, the motorists began to make their way back onto the scene. Cars gradually retook the parkway. I got a feeling that I was close to waking up. It seemed the nightmare was over. I knew that I would come out of this nightmare with a smile.

I stood at the street corner. I saw animals darting in and out of traffic.

Spring was in the air. All seemed normal again.

When suddenly I heard in the distance, a thunderous roar. The rumble moved closer as I swung to my left. Amazingly, there it was. A gigantic herd of deer was making its way up the parkway. The ones in front were oblivious to anything in their path. Each one of them was chewing on some kind of vegetation.

They appeared more and more ominous as they came closer and closer. I knew that if I did not get out of the way, I would be trampled.

Once again I sat up in my bed. This lurch was the final time. I looked around to make sure that I was not being stampeded. I thought briefly in horror about the animals and said to myself ..." how absurd!"

I looked out of my window at the parkway. I could see clearly by the full moon. No deer were forthcoming. The image was still with me. Just like the purplish clouds from the night before, the image would not go away.

XXII-V

So I sat there waiting. Soon there would be daybreak. I watched the clouds divide. A moon shadow touched the half-lit sun; then faded off and died. The most eerie thing about my dream was its elapsed time. Normally when I have a dream, its frame of time is concurrent with the actual length of my dream sequence. This dream oddly, recounted a period of approximately one year.

I was as awestruck by the dream as I was by my ability to give rise to it. I searched my thoughts for some kind of translation. But those images held no significance. I passed it off as the workings of an overactive imagination. Nothing that I rationalized could explain such an absurd apparition.

XXII-V

Many years passed, and the results of that dream were as yet unclear. Whenever I attempted to recall it, my image of the herd would cause a sensation of constant movement. It is a feeling with which I am very familiar. I get it after travelling the approximately nine hundred miles from my parents home to my grandparents up north. When I reach my destination and settle down to rest, I still have the sensation of moving. It takes about five hours to adjust to the condition of stillness. My eyes and ears tell me that I am not moving. Yet, the pressure on my brains and the feeling in my extremities tell me that I am. It is unsettling. When I close my eyes I can still see the highway in front of me. I can still feel the spinning wheels beneath me. And I can see the white lines that help keep me in my lane. Each time I revivify the dream, those feelings are revived as well. It feels as if I had just finished a days drive.

Most striking of all, I could not forget the face of the lead animal. It sounds odd; yet, I had no idea why. It was as if I had known him from somewhere. Looking at this through the new me and my experiences with a certain group of people, I am able to shed new revelations upon the dream. Up to the point where I made contact with Big Bobby, Mr. Long, Jean and others, there was a void in my methodology. My deductive reasoning did not cover all transgressions. In other words, I lacked the ability to draw a precise conclusion. In this post-shelter era, there are certain realities which I cannot escape.

The lead deer I saw was unlike the other ones. He seemed to have some kind of significance. So the other day when a man was picking up cigarettes from the bus stop, it dawned on me. The bull deer looked remarkably like a man whom I stumbled upon in Maryland. It was a week or so before the end of the school year, and I was working hard on my final exams.

It was a Saturday morning. I had taken the bus downtown to the public library. As I waited for the facility to open, I patiently leaned against the building. I thought nothing of the pile of boxes and old papers on the ground behind me. Suddenly they began to move. Then, just as I suspected a man dressed in ragged clothes crawled from underneath. The first words he spoke were cursing at me. He was accusing me of standing on top of him. Then his mood softened. He asked me if could spare a little change.

I stared at him and shrugged my shoulders. Then I tossed some coins on the ground. I said to him…"If anybody needs change it is you." I was so appalled by the man it never crossed my mind that he and I are of the same maker. Though different in nature, we are god's creatures. My next request of him was…"Now get the hell out of here."

Now, with the new experiences being a part of me, my actions were plucking away at my ego. My mortal soul was asking me if I really needed to have been cruel. Did the man deserve what I said to him? I can say today that there is no justification for the insults. His condition was insulting enough.

His demeanor was just that; demeanor. It served only to amplify his problems more when I pushed him. If our roles had been reversed, I would have been asking him for help. It was a request for assistance, and I could not relate to that.

It's all clear now. The the lead elk was the persona of the man beneath the boxes. His bullish attitude brought attention to his unlikely presence. No one would pay attention to him but for his assertive ways. The last elk were representations of his terrible plight. It is obvious that someone has to bring up the rear. I should have known that everyone could not pursue life's goals with success. The weaker, smaller, or less fortunate may fall behind. Some unforgivable factors had lowered his odds of survival. God forbid that it was me who pushed him over the edge.

I will not go so far as to say that I am happy about my recent experiences. Rather, I suggest that I am better off for the exposure. I believe that I am wiser and that I am smarter. Now that I recognize those feelings of disdain which I held for my fellow man, I can relate more closely to these new feelings of empathy. This status opens a door to clearer thinking.

I often addressed the cycles of wealth and poverty as something that was constantly at my doorstep. A more perceptive view shows that it is a formidable part of nature.

For example we might consider the discovery of the Pharaoh's cat. Its tomb was unearthed with many servants, and a fortune in gems. Then there are the kittens that were born behind the dumpster around back. Who will feed them? There are wealthy pet owners whose pure bred dogs vie for blue ribbons at the kennel club. There are also mangy curs being scooped up and taken to the dog pound. Won't someone save them?

And no one can overlook those people who have billions of dollars to spend. Their chauffer driven limousines whizzing past a fellow whose grocery cart is packed with aluminum cans. Will he become a tycoon one day?

Such are the facts of life which help us to thrive. There are always goals that we see as attainable. We strive by any means to move towards them. Though our environs set impediments in our way, we must by our nature continue to struggle.

The universe holds wonders that can be ours in the end. Every creature is blessed with the tools to live for that future. Our innate conditions propel us forward. We perceive this manner as normal. That which is normal for one creature appears as its usual way to other creatures.

We see nature in its present capacity, as it has always been. We may construe other facsimiles. Despite man's overwhelming successes and failures, the seasons still change. The winds still waft across our planet. And the waters still rise and fall.

Mortal beings inhabit the earth unperturbed. We flow with natural affairs, just as the creator intended. We have to believe that such conditions have always been the norm.

All along the food chain, some creatures rise to the top and some fall behind. There is no burning secret. The affairs of man have always known the scrutiny of society at-large. His ways may be cultivated and charted, yet he follows the natural course. No individual can be shielded from the light of truth. Man's ascension to the top of his society is nature's truth.

Man's feelings about cultural status are essential to the ways that we function in nature. One of our major tenets is the separation of people into various classes. Though most citizens may not prefer it, history shows this to be the norm.

Without further adieu, let us delve into man's STRATA OF POPULATIONS. We will begin at layer number five and work our way up to number one.

Our sidewalk sleeper is just one component of this fifth segment. I will label his group layer number five [After the Parade]. When the pomp and circumstances are over; when all the glitter is long since disappeared, this group picks up the scraps. For them, quality of life is not at all an issue. But because life is long, they must show the affects of going through the motions. They must at least appear to be keeping up. Their presence may not be objectionable if they stay outside the realm of contact.

The next segment resembles more closely, general society. This is layer four [Lower Class Status]. This is the hardest working class of citizens. It is upon their backs that all nations have arisen. When each morning comes, they can look forward to a full day of hard labor. These are servants, sweepers, peons, slaves, prisoners of war, and so forth. Upon their backs were built the great wonders of the world. From this class of people came those who pulled the blocks into the great pyramids. They set the bricks in great walls of China. They raised the giant columns of the Parthenon. And they laid the concrete for Roman highways. Those labors, as well as much more that I have not cited can be attributed only to this class of citizens.

The next group is another important historical class. I designate them as layer number three [Tradesman and Engineer Status]. This has been the most fluid of classes. In earlier stages it consisted of artisans, alchemists, magicians, holy men, storytellers, etc. This is the group of citizenry which later developed mathematicians and architects. They designed archway bridges, calculated the Aztec Calendar, built ancient war machines, and constructed life sustaining aqueducts.

And now let us regard what has been the most traditional of the classes. It is at layer two [Nobles (Upper) Echelon]. These are Lords and Ladies; Barons, Knights, Samurai, and chieftain. This is the class which claimed ownership. Whether it was land, property, or other people; it had to be owned by someone within this group. They were traditionally entitled to anything which other nobility did not already own.

The members of this final category have their own separate recognizable status. They are the gods on earth. I label this last group layer one [Vanity Heirs]. These are Kings, Queens, Emperors, Czars, Pharaohs and Caesars. I have excluded Popes from this class, only because they are not succeeded by their offspring. This is the class which gives us our history by their person. No one may ogle Vanity Heirs.

Class status is not easily renounced. Its historical rigidity is evidence of that. Differences of heredity and ethnicity may further compound the the problems of culture. Though our modern world is wiser and has a better understanding, nature's laws nevertheless must be observed. Every society requires a ruling body, enforcement of laws, and common workers.

It is the responsibility of rulers to eliminate despair in its culture. Choices are often based on a person's low or high status. Who you are, as they say, is exactly who you are. Rules have to be imposed. Structure needs to be maintained in cycles of both good and bad times.

XXV

I survived a profound and surprising period of contact with a failing group. I certainly am not the first in history to do so. I went into it with the notion of finding inexpensive room and board. As innocent as it may seem, this motive is what initiated my strife. What I got into was a quality of life that peened my sensibility. It even caused me to wonder at times if I was there as a result of the flow of events, or if it was due to some personal shortcoming.

Such pessimistic thoughts were few, and sort lived. All things considered, I was able to move steadily on my course. This distraction I confess was a bump in the road. But rather than causing apathethy, it stimulated my brain.

I was hearing people say negative things about me. Nowadays when I see friends from my old neighborhoods, it is clear that things are not the same.

Some ask me if I am taking good care of myself. Some want to know if things are still the same as before. And still others laugh in my face.

They have no clue what I have achieved. I can see them going through the daily routines of life. The same horseshoes that they were throwing when I hung around with them are the ones that they retrieved and now throw the other way. It's just a silly game.

Some, who know the sting of hard times, are eager to welcome me back. Others are not so sure. Their chit chat about me has been less than generous. I can sense their desire to throw me to the curb. They dread being exposed to the idea that they too can fall outside this comfortable zone.

A worldly trait I learned from my buddy Jean is that he never cared about what people said about him. Even though the small talk was known to him, Jean never let that aspect of people be a factor. He knew what he had to do. That is what's important.

I grew up in neighborhoods which had more to do with cultural logistics than with personal wishes. Their moods and tones appear now to matter least of all to me.

I should refer to those former neighbors as just another facet of my upbringing. Their attitudes are a preview of how I once saw life. Their attitudes also show a personality which I sought to escape. Culture was based essentially on how well I could please this clique. I recognize something more this time around. It seems the path we are on goes in one predictable direction. If I continue my alliance with this minimized network, I will never discover my full capacity.

Allowing for the shortcomings, I am more comfortable around them still than I am with my brethren from the patio. I am in the process of blazing a new path. The patio group of neighbors will soon lose their need to keep pace with me. Sparks dropped by to tell me about a plan some of them have to move to Florida. He says that there are more state run benefits. He will contact his cousin who is already living with assistance.

I wished him well, but I still cannot see how that would be better. It only serves to perpetuate his blameless outlook. The higher the quality of assistance, the less likely he will need to reach for a higher status.

I had grown more than weary of their motives. It should have been apparent when they bragged, that I did not prefer what they were up to. Still, none cared what I thought. After a period of three months, not one had a job. I was in no position to relocate, but they forced me to consider it.

My easy times on the rental assistance program was in its sixth and final month. It means that I will pay more. But more importantly, it means the counselors will no longer be watching me. I also found out that their on-site office was in the process of closing down. Sparks and the boys would have to find other options. I'm sure they were not left out in the cold. But as I say, I did not care.

That cloud of low stature which hung over me was finally lifted. In all honesty, it was lifted from the entire complex. Some of the guys moved on. Others fought the system until they were legally evicted. Ours soon became a neighborhood of blue collar people living in a work-a-day world.

These were soothing times for me. I started to gather my senses. I would cut my losses, and forget about that tone of impending doom.

My ambitions consisted of getting a cell phone, and a wide screen television. Some of this technology was new to me at the time. I was more familiar with electrical and land line transmissions, transistor circuits, and cablevision than with satellite technology. I was curious about them because I had no global positioning components. I needed them because my other toys had become outdated.

I wanted a cell phone also because everybody else had one. It is another perk of the new millennium. I do not possess a gift of gab. I need however, to be in touch.

I have decided that a cell phone is more of a plaything than a necessity. It tends to make you ignore other people around you. As well as, it causes people to ignore automobile traffic. For me, cell phones have no redeeming cultural values at this point.

Much of the technology which exists today predates our need for it. Until such time as gadgets can refine our social etiquette, having a cell phone is simply keeping up with the Joneses.

Having a laptop computer, in my opinion is a different matter altogether. A lot of us delve into baseless online issues. For me, word processing features are of great satisfaction. I intend to avail myself of all their functions.

Satellite technology has made the world a smaller place. It is virtually possible to find anything you're looking for. Conversely, the opportunity for corruption is available like never before. Satellite communications has proven to be a test of moral standards. Morality in this era is being manipulated to suit men's purposes. As we see cultural and traditional values become less important, I am beginning to wonder which of our traits will come to the fore. Fewer occupations today are being held to a high moral standard. More often than not we are seeing people renege on their obligations to society.

Slothfulness is no longer frowned upon. No one looks for a job that requires hard labor. We call someone lazy only when he absolutely refuses to lift a finger.

Lustfulness is a common thing today. All of our television and computer directories show lustful situations. It is common knowledge that sex sells.

Fraud takes a back seat to none of the above. Citizens are thoughtlessly scammed out of billions of dollars. Since the turn of the century, several mega corporations have been prosecuted for fraudulent financial practices.

This apartment represents a new deal for me. I am getting another chance to prevail. I must choose this path carefully. There is no place for random choices. I will rely more heavily upon my own innate wisdom. There are ways which are not apparent to the untrained eye. We must be careful how we try to affect those ways. Technology and the world are evolving faster than we can adjust.

When I hear people proclaim that we have mastered the world my reaction is that we have not. They say that we no longer face all the ancient paranoia that has plagued mankind. My reaction is that we have only begun to realize how constrained we are to our planet.

Our struggle is with ourselves. It is part of man's physiological structure to be enamored with his persona. He subsequently will draw conclusions about his deeds such as "... we have conquered the world."

Narcissism is a trait which the Greeks brought to our attention thousands of years ago. We have been slow to grasp the significance. It is a term that was derived from the name of a romantic Greek boy named Narcissus. His story is retold in order to exemplify how fragile is the human ego. As the story goes Narcissus fell in love with his own reflection in a pond of water. He was so enamored with the person he beheld that he never left the pond again.

Much of our technological advances are to the benefit of society. The existence of narcissism warns us of another benefit. It is feasible that some technological advancement benefits only our self image.

Some of our ideas are plucked from the very heart of narcissism. It perpetuates ambition and spurs creativity. There should be motive enough to insure basic needs such as comfort, food, and safety. But man will always have to struggle with other things in his head.

When the day comes that we can stare down our noses at the galaxy and say "...we have mastered the universe", maybe then there will be peace.

The great availability of gadgets in reality reflects our propensity for going in circles. Whether we like it or not, there will always be advances. We ultimately will create such a stockpile of technology, that we won't have a need for the people around us.

"Narcissus"... the boy in the reflecting pool.

There will be people in daily life who dream of scientific achievement. They are eager to pursue their far-ranging goals. They do so according to nature's urgings.

There are still others among us who are inclined to more rational beliefs. They look to nature to solve our daily problems. By offsetting the desire to reconfigure nature, some people want to find answers in divine authority. They seek to stem the tide of arrogance.

This is not a choice which individuals have made. We are only reacting to intellectual stimuli. One has to shoot his best shot. As members of a social pecking order we must choose a path which has some significance. We must behave according to what we believe. For this and many other reasons, our lives go in circles. Nothing is new.

That being said; some will aver that it is not too late! We are not yet at the point of no-return. They believe we can leave a functioning earth to those who will live five generations from now.

Other pessimists say that ours are the 'end of days'. They say that our timeless planet has become a fragile orb. Star gazers nowadays only see man made satellites.

Man as a species existing on the earth is in a negative phase. He is as close to being all-powerful as he perceives himself to be. Yet, he has to gather food and he must construct shelter just as all beasts do. We are temporal beings. We are in conformity with nature's galactic cycles. As a result, we exist in evolution as part of this earthly orbit.

Our individual lives are made heavenly by instances of divine intervention. This aspect places us above other creatures. It has made us the superior species. Our spiritual instances can raise an individual to a positive phase. Man has no competition for provisions on this earth. The only thing he has to fear is his cultural rival.

Our entire life's experiences are a balance of this dichotomy: negative and positive. We are touched in folklore by images of Armageddon; the end of the earth. We are bombarded with tales of dire future events. Conversely, we are told of optimistic outcomes. Our sensibilities are candid with hopes of eternal bliss. Our realities are set adrift with predictions of both good and evil.

Thus we ponder our status in the scheme of nature. We try to figure out how to live in all realms. We are obliged to do our bests to find answers to all extremes. We wrestle with day versus night; bleakness versus clarity; and dark heartedness versus light heartedness. In so doing we have committed ourselves to understanding that man in the reflecting pool.

CLOSING

"I" the individual, am blessed with being in limited charge of my circumstances. My complex nature is fundamental to controlling my own destiny. I purport to reveal the truth as it occurs from a living perspective.

The society which I inhabit appears to me be dumbfounded. Our daily lives are enthralled in limbo. We hope that education and technology will spare us from evil doers of the world. Here is a need to define every man. We can only pray that their actions will comport with our ways. We are given this day and a purpose to make it good. Our playground is a much smaller place than at any other time in history. We cannot presume the motives of others. We can only hope that all will be directed toward the common good. There is hardly room today for selfish agendas. Yet some stare down their noses at the muddling crowds.

The slightest difference in political or cultural tenets can have global repercussions. In these unsure times we wrestle with issues of insider versus outsider. There is no final answer. We must continue to redefine ourselves and what we believe.

We are in eternal defiance of the path; still in this way of moral vilification. Our ability to be humane is sometimes maligned by human vanity. Every man is at risk of being judged. Let us not surrender him to the dark hearted fortifications of our temporal means.

ABOUT THE AUTHOR

James Alpheus Frazier was born in Savannah Georgia and a member of the baby boomers generation. There is where he attended public schools. His abilities in athletics earned him scholarships to college. His good grades earned offers in academics. He chose instead to attend junior college while living with relatives in New York. He eventually accepted a basketball grant to a college in Baltimore. He majored in English Literature where his greatest interests reside. After graduating as a dean's list student, he went back to Georgia and became a radio journalist. He joined his brother and others once again in New York where he was a H.S. teacher for nine years. It was later in Georgia however that his lifelong ambition to be a writer took its current identity. James abandoned all the ideas he contrived while living in NYC and let DEER ON THE PARKWAY come into frame.

This is a semi-autobiographical narrative about events which overwhelmed the life of the author. In the midst of a burgeoning career in New York, James Al receives a phone call one day advising that his parents in Georgia had been hospitalized. As the youngest of seven siblings, he realizes that only he is in a position to drop everything and move home. James Al relates how the rose scented world he knew soon fell apart. In his role as caregiver, he is unable to control everything which circumstances are throwing his way. The narrator eventually finds himself in a rut which he never dreamed was possible. Join him as he journeys through his past experiences and recognizes what it will take to pull himself up and away from personal despair. James Al is able to draw parallels between his own upbringing and the strength needed to persevere. See how the world around him functions both as his friend and as his detractor. Only time and inner strength will get him through. His is a story to be shared. James Al is able to recourse the worst of tragedies and make his own personal triumph.

...Soon there would be daybreak. I watched the clouds divide.
A moon shadow touched the half-lit sun; then faded off and died...

Lightning Source UK Ltd.
Milton Keynes UK
UKHW012044260221
379474UK00001BA/31